The Economics of Overlapping Free Trade Areas and the Mexican Challenge

Ronald J. Wonnacott

Canadian-American Committee

Sponsored by
- C.D. Howe Institute (Canada)
- National Planning Association (U.S.A.)

This book is printed on recycled, acid-free paper.

Canadian Cataloguing in Publication Data

Wonnacott, Ronald J., 1930–
    The economics of overlapping free trade areas
and the Mexican challenge

(CAC ; 60)
Sponsored by C.D. Howe Institute (Canada), National Planning
Association (U.S.A.).
Includes bibliographical references.
ISBN 0-88806-284-2

1. Free trade - North America. 2. Free trade. 3. North America -
Economic integration. 4. Customs unions. I. Canadian-American
Committee. II. C.D. Howe Institute. III. National Planning Association.
IV. Title. V. Series.

HF1713.W65 1991   382'.71'097   C91-094915-8

To Yvonne and all those in the
Economics Department at the University of Western Ontario
who have provided such expert and good-humored support.

Contents

Foreword

The speed with which a free trade agreement between Canada, the United States, and Mexico has moved from a dim and distant prospect to the subject of serious trilateral negotiations is startling. This initiative is clearly of enormous importance for three reasons. First, it is a cornerstone of Mexico's efforts to reorient its economy in an outward-looking, market-driven manner. Second, it represents an opportunity to extend the principles of the Canada-U.S. Free Trade Agreement — an unprecedented liberalization of bilateral trade — to North America's other major economic power. And, third, it may mark a major step in a march toward free trade throughout the Western Hemisphere.

As Ronald J. Wonnacott points out in this study, however, the political urgency surrounding the negotiations risks leaving a key decision to be made virtually by default. Should we opt for an expanding multilateral free trade area, or adopt a system of over-lapping bilateral agreements in a "hub-and-spoke" system centered on the United States? This decision would set a precedent with profound implications for the future of trade in the Americas.

An expanding free trade area would extend the benefits of free trade to all its members on a nondiscriminatory basis. A hub-and-spoke system would confer additional benefits on the "hub" country at the expense of its bilateral partner "spokes". Professor Wonnacott observes that even the apparent beneficiary of such a system, the United States, might be worse off in the long run, as the resulting fragmented trading system would hamper the economic growth of its partners, foster protectionist lobbies, and stir political resentment. Based on these considerations, he argues that the cause of free trade in the Western Hemisphere would be much better served by an enlarged free trade agreement.

In sponsoring this study, the Canadian-American Committee continues its long-standing effort to improve general understanding of the importance of international trade to the prosperity of Canada and the United States, and to promote trade policies that enhance the economic wellbeing of both countries. The views expressed in

this study, however, are those of the author; its publication by the
Canadian-American Committee does not imply that all Committee
members endorse all of the author's arguments. The Committee
believes, however, that Professor Wonnacott's views on the key
importance of the type of trading system emerging from the Can-
ada-U.S.-Mexico negotiations deserve attention both from the negotiators themselves and from anyone concerned about the future of
the world trading system.

John P. Fisher   Robert G. Nichols
Co-Chairman   Co-Chairman

Acknowledgments

For their helpful comments on the issues addressed in this study, I am indebted to the those participating in the conference sponsored by the C.D. Howe Institute and the National Planning Association in Washington, D.C., on October 22, 1990; to the participants of three workshops, one at the University of Rochester and two at the University of Western Ontario; and to reviewers from the Canadian-American Committee and the C.D. Howe Institute.

In particular, I wish to thank John Cleghorn, David Iwasu, Ron Jones, Carsten Kowalczyk, Ann Krueger, Jim Markusen, Jim Melvin, Peter Morici, Gordon Ritchie, Bill Robson, Jeffrey Schott, Murray Smith, Daniel Schwanen, John Whalley, and Ian Wooton for their comments, although they should not be held responsible for the views expressed here. I am also indebted to Vince Gray and Brian Rivard for their assistance in acquiring information on trade flows.

Ronald J. Wonnacott
London, Ontario
May 1991

Summary

This study examines the complex issue of trade liberalization in the Americas, and poses the questions: Where do we want to go? and How do we get there? Its chief finding is that it is in the interests of all countries in the hemisphere to ensure that future liberalization in the Americas not be via an inefficient "hub-and-spoke" configuration in which the United States, as the hub, has separate bilateral free trade agreements with Canada and Mexico, but instead via an expanding free trade agreement (FTA). With that agreement, the three countries would be creating an open market with a combined GNP of more than US$6 trillion and with annual trade in goods and services between its members exceeding $270 billion. Such an agreement, moreover, would set the stage for further moves toward a free trading hemisphere from the Beaufort Sea to Cape Horn.

This means that the Canadian, Mexican, and U.S. governments have set the appropriate objective for their 1991 negotiations — namely, a trilateral FTA. Any attempt to change that objective to a simpler Mexico-U.S. bilateral should be strongly resisted because of the hub-and-spoke pattern that would take root.

The Economics of a Hub-and-Spoke System versus an Expanding FTA

Under an expanding FTA, each U.S. partner, such as Canada, would expect: (1) the gains from free trade with the United States, *augmented by* (2) the later, additional gains from free trade with new partners, such as Mexico, as each signs into the expanding FTA. On the other hand, in a hub-and-spoke system, each U.S. partner would achieve essentially the same gains from trade in (1) when signing its own bilateral with the United States; each partner would, however, not get the full gains of (2) — indeed, it could possibly even incur losses — as the United States goes on to sign bilaterals with new spoke partners.

To illustrate, if the United States, with its Canadian bilateral now in place, goes on to sign a bilateral agreement with Mexico, Canada would not achieve the FTA benefits of free access to the Mexican market; instead, its access would worsen because of the discrimination it would face in the Mexican market in competition with U.S. products. (Canadian exports to Mexico would still have to pay a Mexican tariff, whereas U.S. exports to Mexico would not.) Moreover, Canadian firms would have difficulty competing for another reason: they would not get the FTA benefits of less expensive duty-free Mexican inputs that would make them more competitive in world markets. Instead, they would have to face stronger competition in North America and elsewhere from U.S. firms that would be able to acquire these low-cost inputs.

The more spoke bilaterals the United States were to add, the wider the discrimination and the greater the consequent erosion of gains a U.S. partner would have to face. It is even conceivable that a partner's initial gains from its own bilateral FTA with the United States could be more than offset by second-stage costs down the road, leaving it worse off than before this process began. On the other hand, it is also possible that a partner's second-stage costs could be more than offset if the analysis is broadened to take into account the indirect spillover benefits it might receive from increasing its exports to the expanding, more prosperous markets of each new spoke. But whether an existing partner would benefit or lose overall once these second-stage effects are taken into account, one conclusion stands out: it would benefit more from an expanding FTA.

What would happen to the U.S. hub as it adds new spoke partners? It would acquire the benefits of free trade with each new spoke; in particular, it would gain from an expanding domain of preferences in each spoke market in competition with all other spokes. These preferences, based on the fact that the United States alone would have free trade with all spoke countries, would provide it with a substantial advantage in attracting investment. This can be seen from another point of view: any FTA provides a location advantage for participating countries. In a hub-and-spoke system, the United States alone would fully realize this advantage because it alone would be participating in all the free trade bilaterals.

As an example of the special set of preferences the United States would enjoy, a spoke bilateral with Mexico would give the United States preference in the Mexican market in competition with Canada. At the same time, its bilateral with Canada would give it preference in the Canadian market in competition with Mexico. As the United States adds more spoke bilaterals, it would benefit from more and more of these preferences. But in comparison with an FTA, any such U.S. gain would come at even greater expense to its bilateral partners.

Why, then, would there be any new applicants for spoke status — that is, new countries seeking a bilateral with the United States? One answer is that a prospective new spoke country may, of course, be short-sighted, seeing only the immediate benefits of free trade with the United States and not the subsequent buildup of costs. There is, however, a more fundamental reason that it might be willing to say yes — since it would have an incentive to do so even if it were to foresee fully the accumulating costs and, indeed, even if it were to be in the special situation in which these costs, down the road, would exceed its initial free trade gains. The reason is that essentially all the new spoke's decision would do is give it benefits of free trade with the United States. If it says yes, it would get these benefits; if it says no, it would not. It will have to face the costs of being discriminated against as the United States goes on to add new spokes — whether or not it decides to participate in this process.

Existing Trade Patterns in the Hemisphere

When this theory is confronted with empirical evidence on hemi-spheric trade patterns, it is clear that each country's primary interest is in getting free trade with the United States. This follows not only from the technological benefits but also because the United States is, almost without exception, the largest trading partner of every country in the Americas. Moreover, when a country gets free trade with the United States, its percentage income gains can be very large, running well into triple digits, even if it closes only a small proportion of the present productivity gap between itself and the United States.

The evidence does not provide a firm fix on how much an existing spoke might be damaged if the United States were to add more spokes; indeed, if anything, it suggests that an existing spoke may not be damaged at all if one takes into account the indirect spillover benefits from the large income increases that may occur in the new spokes. The evidence does, however, leave intact the most important conclusion of this study: a hub-and-spoke system would be clearly inferior to an expanding FTA.

The evidence further suggests that a hub-and-spoke system would not distort and damage existing trade as much as future trade. One reason for this is that existing two-way trade between, say, Canada and Mexico is now so small — only about US$2 billion in 1989, versus Canada-U.S. trade of over US$170 billion. Thus, an FTA is important for a country such as Canada not so much because it would prevent damage to its existing sales in Mexico, but because it would prevent damage to its future sales in this rapidly expanding market.

The Canadian Interest

There are several specific reasons why Canada should favor the negotiation of an expanding free trade area, rather than standing aside and allowing a hub-and-spoke system to develop. First, it is better for Canada to acquire gains from, for example, comparative advantage and economies of scale by participating in an expanding FTA than to face the costs of an expanding hub-and-spoke network that would discriminate against Canadian exports and make it difficult for Canadian firms to remain competitive. Second, a trilateral negotiation would better allow Canada to protect its interests — for example, by ensuring an appropriate treatment of the Maquiladoras to prevent them from artificially attracting industry and distorting North American trade and investment. Third, an FTA negotiation would mean that Canada would not be sideswiped by a Mexico-U.S. bilateral giving Mexico better access to the U.S. market than Canada enjoys.

Indeed, it can be argued that Canadians have little choice but to participate in the upcoming trilateral FTA negotiations. In a sense, it does not even matter whether they believe an FTA would benefit Canada or not. As long as the United States and Mexico are going forward with a negotiated agreement, it is worse for Canada to stay away and not participate. In this respect, it is like the Canadian decision to participate in the Uruguay Round: it did not matter whether Canadians liked the idea or not; it would have been worse to stay away. One reason is common to both cases: the high cost of being an outsider when trading partners are liberalizing their trade.

The Mexican Interest

Mexico should reject a hub-and-spoke development for precisely the same reasons. Once it becomes a U.S. free trade partner, it will find itself in exactly the same situation as Canada: facing losses from discrimination as the United States goes on to sign hub-and-spoke bilaterals with other countries, such as Chile or Venezuela. For example, Mexico should ask: If the United States continues to extend its free trade domain with a sequence of tailored spoke bilaterals rather than within the discipline and consistency imposed by an expansion of an FTA, what is to prevent Mexico from being sideswiped down the road by a U.S. concession of better access to some other Latin American country?

The U.S. Interest

There are also reasons why a hub-and-spoke is not in the interest of the United States, even though it would be the apparent beneficiary because of the special preferences it would receive. Offsetting these benefits, however, would be the costs to the United States — as well as to Canada and Mexico — since, compared with an FTA, income would be lost throughout the hemisphere because of trade distortions and associated inefficiencies such as excess transport and administrative costs and rent-seeking waste. These would be compounded by the almost certain inconsistencies inherent in spoke bilaterals.

The United States also has broader political and economic reasons for rejecting a hub-and-spoke system. Because of its central geographic location and economic size, the United States would dominate any trading system in the Americas. It would not be in its foreign policy interest to be seen as further dominating the economic activity of its neighbors by participating in the development of a hub-and-spoke trading structure that would leave markets in the

Americas carved up into a patchwork of what the United States would view as preferences but which its partner countries would justifiably view as discrimination. Because the preferences built into such a system would benefit the United States at the expense of its partners in the hemisphere, hub-and-spoke bilaterals would not be an "equal opportunity" partnership. The level-playing-field argument, so often abused in other contexts in the past, could then be used with considerable justification against the United States, because the rules of the trading regime itself would be biased in its favor. There are already many voices claiming that even past non-discriminatory trade has allowed the United States to exploit other nations in the hemisphere. A discriminatory hub-and-spoke system could provide these charges with a degree of legitimacy that they now do not deserve.

Another U.S. problem in a hub-and-spoke regime would arise if there were more applicants for a U.S. bilateral than U.S. negotiating resources could accommodate. The United States would then be forced to discriminate — in saying yes to some countries, no to others — in offering a negotiation that would itself be discriminatory.

A final disadvantage of a hub-and-spoke regime for the United States is that this system could strengthen U.S. protectionism, thereby weakening the prospects for worldwide trade liberalization. The reason is that the U.S. administration, the major promoter and supporter of multilateral free trade in the past, might encounter increased resistance from U.S. business interests because such trade would strip away the special preferential benefits they would be getting from a hub-and-spoke system. This raises the possibility that a hub-and-spoke configuration might encourage a new U.S. protectionism that would seek to protect U.S. firms from foreign competition, not just in the domestic U.S. market as always, but *also in the markets of spoke countries* where U.S. exporters would be protected by preferential treatment. The problem with such a new U.S. "domestic-export protectionism" is that it might be able to disguise itself as free trade because it would be the defense of a set of existing free trade agreements. But it would still be a dangerous form of protectionism, insofar as it could be used to resist the two more appropriate objectives of U.S. trade policy — namely, an expanding FTA and multilateral free trade.

What Does This Mean for the North American Free Trade Negotiations?

Canada, the United States, and Mexico must remain firm in their present commitment to negotiate free trade in the framework of an expanding trilateral FTA rather than the hub-and-spoke system that would result from a Mexico-U.S. bilateral. This commitment to an expanding FTA is particularly important for the United States because it holds the negotiating key. As the recipient of applications by new countries for bilaterals, it is in a position to refuse, leaving them with the option of joining the existing FTA instead.

Although it is essential to maintain the trilateral framework in the current negotiations with Mexico, certain specific bilateral provisions can still be accommodated on a temporary basis — subject to a clearly defined phase-out schedule — or even on a permanent basis on issues that, by their very nature, are exclusively bilateral and must remain so, no matter how many countries might be included in the future. Examples might be Mexico-U.S. agreements on migration or on very low-wage transborder services. Such agreements would raise no hub-and-spoke problems as long as they had no discriminatory effect on existing or future partners. (This study neither recommends nor rejects these policies; they simply illustrate issues that are inherently bilateral.) It is only on potentially discriminatory issues such as tariff removal that the trilateral binding need apply.

Another negotiating guideline is that the existing FTA — at present the Canada-U.S. FTA, but perhaps a Canada-Mexico-U.S. FTA by 1993 — should not be renegotiated each time a new applicant nation or group of nations is to be included. Not only might this inflate negotiating costs, but, more importantly, a renegotiation of provisions might drag an FTA back into the political arena of the existing partners.

This seems particularly important for the present Mexican administration, which is now apparently attempting to lock in trade and other reforms that cannot easily be reversed by future governments. Mexico should have a substantial interest in setting a precedent now that will insulate its own free trade agreement from being reopened in the future.

Finally, suppose the United States and Mexico were prepared to go further in liberalizing trade than does the Canada-U.S. FTA. While this would not be possible in tariffs, which are already zero in the Canada-U.S. FTA, it might be possible in some other areas — for example, government procurement. But this would generate hub-and-spoke contamination of the trading system, since existing partner Canada would now be discriminated against in such contracts. To prevent this, such an increased liberalization would have to be trilateralized, but this would require reopening the Canada-U.S. FTA. This would be reasonable under two conditions. First, any change should further liberalize rather than protect. Second, any change must be acceptable to all existing partners — as, for example, the United States and Canada have judged acceptable the recent "reopening" of their FTA to liberalize it further by two rounds of accelerated tariff cuts. Indeed, such a reopening, subject to these two restrictions, would allow the far-from-perfect Canada-U.S. FTA to be improved — an important objective in itself.

Finally, the analysis of trading options in this study should have application far beyond the Western Hemisphere. In particular, it may be useful in establishing economic ties between the European Community, Eastern Europe, and possibly several states emerging from the Soviet Union. Will this development take the form of an expanding common market, or a complex hub-and-spoke system centered on the European Community? Or, perhaps, a whole set of such systems, centered on other hubs as well?

Chapter One

Introduction

The world trading system in early 1991, viewed from a North American vantage point, seems to be at a watershed. The Uruguay Round of multilateral negotiations to liberalize trade has already failed to meet one deadline; although it has now been apparently revived, it is far from clear that it will yield a successful outcome beyond, perhaps, some cobbled-up cosmetic gesture. At least in the multilateral forum, trade liberalization remains an elusive goal. In the absence of substantial, concrete success in the Uruguay Round, the problem may go beyond lost opportunities for more liberalization to further erosion of the liberalization that has, with such effort, been achieved in the past. For example, one risk is that the United States may resort to unilateral action to deal with sensitive issues that have been deferred during the Uruguay Round negotiations.[1]

Traditionally, trade negotiations have been viewed as a way in which a government can establish discipline over its protectionist, domestic special-interest groups. Has this now been turned on its head as special interests — for example, agriculture in Europe and elsewhere — have become strong enough not only to resist this discipline, but to go beyond that to damage and perhaps destroy the trade negotiations themselves? This would be a major — though not laudable — accomplishment, since these special interests simultaneously have had to fight off domestic pressure for reform from overburdened taxpayers and consumers.

---

1 The problem is similar to the one that would have had to be faced if the Canada-U.S. free trade negotiations had failed in 1987. For example, U.S. concern about Canadian duty remissions on auto imports from third countries was deferred on the (correct) expectation that it would be dealt with in the free trade negotiations. Had those negotiations not succeeded, there was a substantial risk of U.S. unilateral action on this and other issues, with potential damage to existing trade patterns.

Multilateral and Regional Trade Liberalization

For Europeans, the focus of attention is increasingly a continental one, because of the creation of "Europe 1992" and the prospect of the assimilation of East European countries. In the Far East, there are numerous regional proposals, with potentially the most significant being led by Japan.

A regional trading bloc is also developing in the Americas. True, the United States has long been a major supporter of the General Agreement on Tariffs and Trade (GATT) and its most-favored-nation concept of nonpreferential multilateral liberalization. But whether or not such multilateral liberalization can again be activated by a revival of the Uruguay Round, regional free trade is being extended in the hemisphere beyond the Canada-U.S. free trade area (FTA) as a result of President Bush's "Enterprise for the Americas" — an initiative that offers Latin American countries some debt forgiveness and a fostering of foreign investment as they liberalize their trade and their economies. A favorable response by some of these countries is now developing, based on:

- their recognition of the benefits of free trade in the hemisphere, especially with the United States;
- their concern that they may be left out of an increasingly protectionist U.S. market in the future;
- the desire of some of their governments to lock in a free market orientation that cannot easily be reversed by succeeding governments; and
- a concern that they may be left behind if a lineup of candidate countries develops.

The first country to accept this challenge is Mexico. In May 1991, the U.S. administration acquired the fast-track authority that allowed it to begin formal negotiations with Mexico and Canada in June 1991, with the negotiations scheduled to be completed by late 1991 or early 1992. Assuming this timetable holds, approval could come in 1992, and the agreement could come into effect by early 1993.

With that agreement, the three countries would be creating an FTA with a combined GNP of more than US$6 trillion, and with annual trade in goods and services between its members exceeding US$270 billion. Moreover, such an agreement would set the stage for further moves toward a free trading hemisphere from the Beaufort Sea to Cape Horn.

An important question is whether we are moving away from the traditional North American view of regional trade liberalization as a policy consistent with and supportive of multilateral liberalization and toward a view of regional liberalization as a policy that is an end in itself, with multilateral liberalization falling by the way. In my view, it is essential to keep regional liberalization in its traditional role of complementing, rather than substituting for, multilateral liberalization. Thus, it is necessary to ensure that any regional liberalization take the most appropriate form. This is especially true if, in the next decade, the major successes in trade liberalization are regional, not multilateral. Keeping regional agreements consistent with multilateral liberalization will be important to ensure that it will be feasible to move later in that preferred multilateral direction. Achieving such consistency will not be easy or automatic, since regional liberalization by its very nature includes elements of both free trade (among partners) and protection (against outsiders, whether or not trade barriers against them are increased). Accordingly, any regional liberalization should be designed to minimize protection and the growth of special-interest groups that will later resist any move to multilateral liberalization.

A number of regional initiatives are now being considered or implemented — for example, the extension of the European Community (EC) to include new countries, the creation of FTAs in the Pacific, and the extension of free trade in North America to the nations to the South. What should such regional liberalization take? In North America, the free trade negotiations with Mexico will establish the pattern for extending trade liberalization throughout the hemisphere. This is a much more complex issue than has traditionally been believed. With Mexico, it is not just the creation of another FTA, with the traditional, well-known economics this implies. Instead, there are two quite different patterns that may develop, one potentially more damaging than the other to future multilateral liberalization, and having less beneficial effects on the participating countries.

The Two Broad Forms of Regional Trade Liberalization

There are two broad approaches the United States can use to establish free trade with other countries in the hemisphere:

- *A plurilateral free trade agreement* in which the United States and the other countries are trading freely, with the borders of each country open equally to trade with each of the others.
- *A system of overlapping free trade areas* — that is, a hub-and-spoke system in which the United States, as the hub in a rimless wheel, has a bilateral spoke agreement with each of the other countries. While the United States would be trading freely with each spoke country, none of the spoke countries would be trading freely with any of the others.[2] See Figure 1, in which straight lines represent the rapidly multiplying trade barriers remaining between the spokes as more are added.

---

2 This hub-and-spoke system is the same "two-sided triangle" that I examined in "Canada's Future in a World of Trade Blocs: A Proposal," *Canadian Public Policy* 1 (Winter 1975): 118–130; and in "Controlling Trade and Foreign Investment in the Canadian Economy: Some Proposals," *Canadian Journal of Economics* 15 (November 1982): 574–576. In 1990, I applied this analysis to the hub-and-spoke system that could develop as a result of negotiations with Mexico (*Canada and the U.S.-Mexico Free Trade Negotiations*, C.D. Howe Institute Commentary 21 [Toronto: C.D. Howe Institute, 1990]). At the same time, Richard G. Lipsey was also addressing the problem independently (see *Canada at the U.S.-Mexico Free Trade Dance: Wallflower or Partner?*, C.D. Howe Institute Commentary 20 [Toronto: C.D. Howe Institute, 1990], pp. 4–5.) Some of the issues that arise in a hub-and-spoke system are also implicit in the discussion of the recontracting problem in Peter Morici, "The Implications for the Future of U.S. Trade Policy," in Peter Morici, ed., *Making Free Trade Work: The Canada-U.S. Agreement* (New York: Council on Foreign Relations, 1990), p. 147. See also Yung C. Park and Jung Ho Yoo, "More Free Trade Areas: A Korean Perspective," in Jeffrey J. Schott, ed., *Free Trade Areas and U.S. Trade Policy* (Washington, D.C.: Institute for International Economics, 1989), pp. 141–158. Park and Yoo describe the hub-and-spoke problem as a star, with the United States at the center and its partner countries at the points.

In considering the possible Mexican and Canadian spokes, it is important not to forget the first U.S. FTA with Israel. However, this was largely a politically motivated agreement. While it does have economic implications that are substantial from the Israeli point of view, it covers a sufficiently small volume of trade to prevent it from disturbing the present analysis.

5

Figure 1: *Two Options for the Development of Free Trade in the Western Hemisphere*

(A)

*One Expanding
Plurilateral Free Trade Area*

(B)

*A Hub-and-Spoke System
of Overlapping Free Trade Areas*

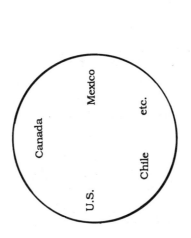

The existing
U.S. bilateral
with Canada...

...followed by
a U.S. bilateral
with Mexico...

...and with
other countries
in the hemisphere.

In this study, the other countries of the hemisphere are referred to as "partner countries", whether they are FTA partners of the United States or spoke countries to the U.S. hub. Obviously, there are many variants in between. For example, another possibility is a hub-and-spoke system in which two of the spoke countries have their own bilateral FTA.

The initial objective in this study is not to examine such variants, but instead to compare these two trading regimes in their simplest forms. They represent two entirely different approaches to liberalizing trade. Because an FTA is far closer than a hub-and-spoke to free trade and because it does not provide one country — in this example, the United States — with the central role it would have in a hub-and-spoke system, these two approaches lead to two very different economic and geopolitical systems. Moreover, it will be shown that there is likely to be far less resistance to multilateral free trade in an FTA than in a hub-and-spoke system.

It is important to identify and understand the differences in those two regimes, because the free trade negotiations with Mexico in 1991 will put in place one of these two patterns. If, following the present objective, all three countries negotiate an expanded North American free trade agreement (NAFTA), the result will be the plurilateral FTA shown in Figure 1. On the other hand, if for some reason — perhaps the pressure of time — the United States and Mexico were to judge that a trilateral agreement could not be reached at this time and were instead to sign their own bilateral agreement, the result would be a hub-and-spoke system, with the United States having separate spoke bilaterals with Canada and Mexico — and quite possibly adding other spoke countries later.

The objective of this monograph is not to provide a detailed brief on the specific provisions — for example, in autos, energy, investment, or whatever — that the United States has negotiated with Canada, may be negotiating with Mexico, or may eventually negotiate with any of the other countries in the Americas or beyond. Instead, the objective is to take a long look forward to where trade in the hemisphere is going. What sort of a trading system do we want in the Americas in 10 to 20 years? Only when that question has been satisfactorily answered will it be possible to make appropriate decisions in the detailed negotiations in 1991.

Clarifying where we want to go will require careful study of the economics of the two broad options shown in Figure 1. This is critical in this threshold period in which the risk of decision by default is high. We are now entering a process in which the negotiators will be faced with a staggering array of negotiating detail. The danger is that they may become so preoccupied with the nuts and bolts, and elected officials so distracted by having to deal with the political opposition to trade liberalization, that both groups may not keep in focus the question: In what direction should we be going in the Americas?

Outline of the Study

An analysis of how an expanding FTA compares with a hub-and-spoke system is important not only for the Americas, but — perhaps even more — for other spheres such as that developing in Western Europe, Eastern Europe, and the new Soviet Union. Accordingly, the next three chapters will be devoted to this analysis, with almost no reference to North America, Europe, or any other specific region.

The simpler form — an FTA — will be analyzed in Chapter 2. Since most of the economics of FTAs have already been published elsewhere, this chapter can essentially be viewed as self-contained, and those already familiar with this topic can quickly pass over it. (There is some new material, for example, on how economies of scale may affect trade diversion.) In addition to describing such concepts as trade diversion, discrimination, and preference, Chapter 2 covers the beneficial free trade effects and damaging protective effects of an FTA. It also shows how an FTA may weaken or strengthen the parallel thrust for multilateral free trade in the GATT. Because of its pros and cons, the judgment on whether any specific FTA is beneficial depends on the characteristics of the participants and the form of their agreement. This chapter also indicates some reasons why both the creation of the bilateral Canada-U.S. FTA and its possible extension to create a trilateral Canada-Mexico-U.S. FTA are expected to have a favorable effect.

Chapter 3 compares a hub-and-spoke system and an FTA. Since the economics of the two regimes are entirely different, a whole new analysis of hub-and-spoke systems, or overlapping free trade areas, is required. Specifically, compared with an FTA, a hub-and-spoke system can be expected to generate special benefits for the hub country and even larger corresponding costs for the spokes, with the hub gaining at its partners' expense and with total collective income reduced.

This comparison of a hub-and-spoke system with an FTA provides a preliminary answer to the question: Where should we be going? It also provides the basis for addressing the other central question in Chapter 3: What happens to all countries involved if a hub-and-spoke system develops from scratch? That is, how does a hub-and-spoke system compare with the status quo? This would be the appropriate question if, in the absence of an FTA option, the United States were to negotiate a bilateral with Mexico and offer only similar bilaterals to other countries.

Chapter 4 addresses a number of additional problems raised by a hub-and-spoke system.

In Chapter 5, the focus shifts to applying this theory to the specific North American case. An examination of the empirical evidence raises the question: Does the choice of including Mexico in an FTA or in a hub-and-spoke matter that much, since the only difference is whether trade between Mexico and Canada is free (in an FTA) or continues to be restricted (in a hub-and-spoke), and the volume of Canada-Mexico trade is so small that it can scarcely matter? The answer is: Yes it does matter, for several reasons — the most obvious being the evidence of strong prospects for future growth in that trade.

Chapter 6 looks at the specific interests of each of the three NAFTA countries — Canada, Mexico and the United States. Of particular concern is the U.S. interest. Even though it is the apparent beneficiary of a hub-and-spoke system, there are several reasons for the United States to reject it.

These first six chapters answer the first broad question: Where do we want to go? Chapter 7 briefly addresses the question: How do we get there? The straightforward answer is to negotiate an expanding FTA; one hopes the issue never becomes more complex than this. However, there are important guidelines for even the simplest form of such a negotiation.

Finally, in addressing possible future developments in Chapter 8, while I make no claim that the hub-and-spoke versus FTA question will be *the* issue in trade policy in the 1990s, it may be, because of the potential for spoke agreements within each hemisphere and perhaps even between hemispheres. For example, it is possible that some form of Japanese-U.S. trade agreement might be considered. Would this make Japan a spoke in the U.S. wheel?

But whether or not history unfolds in this way, there will be other important trade-related issues to address as well, such as the development and international transfer of technology. This monograph examines the liberalization of trade, including the elimination of tariffs and other barriers to trade. (Although the term "tariff" is used throughout this study, the analysis applies to nontariff barriers as well.) While tariffs have become less important over time, other nontariff barriers have become more important. The uncertainty — and hence the damaging effects on investment — from nontariff barriers can be substantial, even if they are seldom if ever used.

Chapter Two

The Economics of a Free Trade Area:
Trade Creation, Diversion, Preference, and Discrimination

A free trade area (FTA) provides member countries with gains from trade as their barriers to trade with each other are removed. Outside countries that are excluded from the FTA are likely to suffer some damage. This exclusion of outside countries will also have an effect on the member countries.

Economic Benefits of an FTA: Trade Creation

As the partners in an FTA eliminate trade barriers among themselves, their expanding trade provides real income benefits from comparative advantage, economies of scale, and more competitive — and hence more efficient — domestic markets. Moreover, a trade agreement often provides a valuable discipline in domestic policy-making; each government has an increased ability to pursue the national interest because it can invoke an agreement that "leaves it no choice" but to reject appeals for protection from special-interest groups that otherwise might be politically irresistible.

So long as purchases in a member country are switched from its own higher-cost domestic producers to lower-cost producers in its FTA partner country, the result is *trade creation*. This benefits members of the FTA[1] without damaging excluded outside countries.

---

1 Under standard assumptions — that is, in the absence of the very special conditions that could make liberalized trade inferior to protection. See footnote 9 in this chapter.

Other Effects of an FTA:
Trade Diversion, Preference, and Discrimination

Trade creation is not the only reason that trade between FTA members — for example, between Canada and the United States — may increase. The United States may switch its previous purchases from a lower-cost source (say, Japan) to a higher-cost partner country (say, Canada), because, under the FTA, the United States favors Canadian goods over Japanese. (It gives free access to its market to Canadian, but not Japanese, goods.) This sort of switch in U.S. purchases is called *trade diversion*, and it involves a cost since the United States is now buying from a higher-cost source.[2] Since trade diversion is important in analyzing both an FTA and a hub-and-spoke trading regime, it will be reviewed briefly with the simplest possible example.

Suppose that, before any FTA is formed, the United States has a 10 percent tariff on an item bought from the Japanese for $100; because of the 10 percent tariff, this items sells in the United States for $110. Suppose Canada is a higher-cost source — say, $104. Before the FTA, Americans do not buy the Canadian item because its price in the United States (including the U.S. tariff) is about $114. But when the FTA is formed, the U.S. tariff on the Canadian item is removed, so Americans can buy it for $104, and do so rather than buy the Japanese good, which continues to sell in the United States for $110 because of the U.S. tariff it still faces. This could cause a reduction in world welfare because production of this good has been switched from Japan to Canada, where the cost of producing it is $4 more.[3] This loss of $4 per unit is borne by the United States: although U.S. consumers save $6 because they are now paying $104 rather than $110, the U.S. Treasury (and hence U.S. taxpayers) loses the $10 duty previously (but no longer) collected. The result is a net loss of $4 to the U.S. taxpayer/consumer. This can be

---

2 For the original discussion of trade diversion and trade creation, see Jacob Viner, *The Customs Union Issue* (New York: Carnegie Endowment for International Peace, 1950).

3 One reason this numerical example is oversimplified is that it assumes that the United States is a price taker. Moreover, possible benefits from trade diversion are not considered; they will be discussed later in this section.

referred to as a "terms-of-trade" loss because the United States is acquiring this good on the international market for $104 rather than the original $100.

While the United States has engaged in *trade diversion* — switching its import purchases from Japan to a higher-cost Canadian source — Canada, the FTA partner, has acquired *preference* in the U.S. market in competition with Japan. (Canadian exports get duty-free access to the U.S. market, but Japanese exports do not.) For precisely the same reason, Japan, as the excluded third country, faces *discrimination* in the U.S. market in competition with Canada. Each of these three italicized terms describes the same phenomenon, as viewed by each of the three countries involved.[4] Of course, any country participating in an FTA will almost certainly be diverting trade in some products while receiving preference in partners' markets in other products.

To sum up so far: A member country in an FTA faces *benefits* from trade creation and from preferences acquired in partners' markets,[5] but *costs* from diverting trade in some products.

Thus, from the argument so far, one cannot say whether or not a participating country will benefit from an FTA without carefully considering its specific circumstances. However, the analysis does not end here; an expectation of net benefit from an FTA is strength-

---

4   In the literature, the term *trade diversion* is often used too broadly to refer to any or all of these three effects. In the specific example cited here, authors may refer correctly to the "cost of trade diversion to the United States" or erroneously to the "cost of trade diversion to Japan." This confusion can be avoided by more specifically referring in this example to U.S. trade *diversion*, Canadian *preference* in the U.S. market, and the *discrimination* Japan faces in the U.S. market.

This example follows the literature by focusing on the direct effects of an FTA, deferring the discussion of its secondary effects — namely, the benefits it could generate for excluded countries because it raises the income of the partner countries in the FTA. The Europeans have often used this argument to answer North American and other criticisms of the European Community (EC). Specifically, the Europeans argue that, although the formation and expansion of the EC has led to discrimination against excluded countries such as the United States and Canada, any depressing effect on their exports has been more than offset by the greater European demand for their exports due to income increases generated by the EC.

5   Preference in partners' markets increases the demand for a country's exports. Under standard assumptions, this raises the domestic price, generating a net gain because the benefit to producers exceeds the cost to consumers.

ened, though far from guaranteed, for three reasons that may make its one potentially costly effect — trade diversion — beneficial rather than damaging.

First, while a member country diverting trade does suffer the terms-of-trade damage cited above, it also benefits from increased efficiency in production and consumption insofar as trade diversion reduces its domestic price toward the world price; in the example above, the initial U.S. domestic price of $110 is reduced to $104, part of the way toward the world price of $100. These trade diversion benefits may even be large enough to offset the terms-of-trade loss, leaving trade diversion, on balance, beneficial.[6]

Second, because trade diversion lowers the domestic price of the item in the United States — from $110 to $104 — it may reduce the size and political influence of the competing domestic U.S. industry. With its political power eroded, the industry may no longer be able successfully to defend its protection against third countries such as Japan. As the U.S. tariff against these countries erodes — suppose, in the limiting case, to zero — then all imports, from Japan as well as from Canada, will enter the United States duty free. U.S. buyers will again purchase from Japan — for $100, rather than for $104 from Canada.[7] In this case, the short-run trade diversion to Canada caused by the FTA disappears in the long run. The efficient purchase from Japan is restored and, indeed, increased because of the lower U.S. domestic price. Thus, what began as trade diversion eventually becomes a *beneficial expansion of efficient trade with a country excluded from the FTA.*

---

6 The term *trade diversion* has two different definitions. This study uses the one that includes both the negative terms-of-trade effect and the positive effects on production and consumption efficiency. The increased efficiency in production induced by the fall in domestic price occurs because high-cost domestic production is displaced by imports; specifically, imports that now cost $104 displace previous domestic production that cost $104 to $110. The increased efficiency in consumption occurs because consumers increase their purchases of bargain-priced imports; specifically, imports that provide consumers with $104–110 of benefit are now purchased for the first time, because consumers can acquire them for only $104.

7 This possibility is described in Martin Richardson, "Trade Diversion and Endogenous Tariff Formation" (Washington, D.C., Georgetown University, Department of Economics, 1990, unpublished manuscript).

Third, if Canada can capture sufficient economies of market size — for example, economies of scale — from the Canada-U.S. FTA, the cost of producing an item in Canada may fall enough — in the example, to less than $100 — to make Canada, the FTA partner, a lower-cost source than outsider Japan. In this case, inefficient trade diversion becomes efficient and is ultimately beneficial for both FTA partners. Moreover, their benefit will exceed the loss to Japan — that is, all three countries will collectively benefit — because the item is now being produced at a lower-cost source.

Thus, trade diversion may not be as damaging as typically believed. Nonetheless, it is still possible for it to be substantial and costly enough to make an FTA, on balance, damaging to a participating country. For the special circumstances that strengthen the expectation that the net effects of the Canada-U.S. FTA would be beneficial for each country and that suggest further net benefits for each participant as Mexico is added, see Appendix 2-1 at the end of this chapter.

Although, for reasons cited above, trade diversion may benefit or damage the countries within an FTA, it will damage excluded countries such as Japan. They will be damaged as FTA members divert their purchases away from Japan and other excluded countries to FTA partners.[8]

An FTA Compared with Multilateral Free Trade

Countries such as Japan that are excluded from an FTA will judge multilateral free trade (MFT) superior because there will be no trade diversion to damage them. Moreover, under standard assumptions, MFT will be collectively superior to an FTA from the point of view of all countries in the world, including both those that are members of the FTA and those that are not. One way of seeing why this is so is to note that under MFT there is unrestricted trade creation and an absence of trade diversion. This means that all goods are produced at their lowest-cost locations; in this sense, the MFT

---

8 The reduced demand for Japanese exports will, under standard assumptions, reduce prices in Japan, thereby damaging Japanese producers more than Japanese consumers benefit.

outcome is efficient, generating the largest collective worldwide real income level.[9]

How does MFT compare with an FTA from the collective point of view of the members of the FTA? Under standard assumptions, along with the assumption that the FTA members cannot improve their terms of trade *vis-à-vis* the rest of the world, MFT will be collectively superior for these countries.[10] The reasons are: (i) MFT provides the same benefits of trade creation as does an FTA, including the benefits from comparative advantage and economies of scale, but it extends them over a broader worldwide domain; and (ii) there is none of the FTA's trade diversion, since there are no excluded countries from which purchases can be diverted. Thus, given these assumptions, an FTA will be collectively inferior for its members to MFT *if MFT can be negotiated.* But if it cannot, an FTA may offer its members collective net benefits and accordingly be the policy they pursue.[11]

---

9 While the collective superiority of MFT over an FTA for all countries follows from standard assumptions, it is possible to find very special assumptions that would make MFT inferior. For example, a very special configuration of trade-distorting domestic taxes that are offset by trade restrictions may make liberalized trade inferior to continued protection. Such a special configuration of domestic taxes could also make MFT inferior to an FTA because MFT involves a greater domain of liberalized trade.

However, it is one thing to solve theoretically for such a very special configuration of trade-distorting taxes; it is quite another to find it in the real world. In particular, note that MFT inferiority does not follow from *any* configuration of trade-distorting domestic taxes, but only from a *very special* configuration of such taxes. Nonetheless, because such conditions might conceivably exist, I hereafter state or imply that the *expectation* is that MFT would be superior to an FTA.

Even if this very special configuration of trade-distorting domestic taxes were to exist, it does not necessarily mean that an FTA leaving these taxes in place would be the best policy to pursue. Instead, the best policy may be MFT and the reform of these taxes.

10 If the FTA countries can influence world prices and their tariffs can accordingly improve their terms of trade, then MFT need no longer be collectively superior for them.

11 There are a number of reasons why it may be difficult to negotiate MFT under the General Agreement on Tariffs and Trade (GATT). The 96 member countries have widely divergent and conflicting interests that are difficult to reconcile, given GATT's *de facto* consensus requirement that allows one or a few countries to block the adoption of new provisions. This means that GATT negotiations are often subject to extended delays and yield an inadequate set of rules. As Jeffrey Schott has noted: "If one deducts all textiles trade...and other exemptions..., nonfactor...

This point can perhaps be summarized by posing the question sometimes used by supporters of a Super-GATT of countries that are able and willing to negotiate free trade among themselves in a world in which free trade by all countries cannot be negotiated: Why should trade liberalization among some countries be blocked because MFT is not feasible, perhaps because other countries cannot participate due to domestic political pressures that are damaging even to themselves? A free trade agreement, whether in the form of a Super-GATT or an FTA, may be a way of unblocking the thrust of two or more countries to achieve trade liberalization. [12] Thus, it may be a way of getting more trade liberalization, while at the same time allowing participating countries to continue to support multilateral free trade in the GATT.

Finally, it should be noted that even in the typical case where an FTA is inferior to MFT for all the FTA members collectively, it is

---

11 - cont'd.

...services, and the trade of non-members of the GATT, as well as trade subject to...voluntary export restraints and more than 200 other...gray area restrictions, only about 60 percent of world trade in goods and services is subject to GATT disciplines" (see "More Free Trade Areas?" in Jeffrey Schott, ed., *Free Trade Areas and U.S. Trade Policy* [Washington, D.C.: Institute for International Economics, 1989], pp. 7–8).

In addition, these inadequate rules are often inadequately enforced. Sometimes, enforcement is difficult because the rules are vague. In other cases, disputing parties — in particular, the United States and the EC — have implicitly used the consensus rule to block GATT decisions. For example, for years the United States delayed conforming to a GATT ruling that required change in its Domestic International Sales Corporation program.

12 An FTA may or may not be a regional grouping. The Canada-U.S. FTA is regional, but the European Free Trade Association is not, nor would a Super-GATT be. If a country such as Chile were to join a Canada-Mexico-U.S. FTA, then the resulting FTA would no longer be regionally circumscribed. Similarities in culture or language may make it more likely that an FTA will be formed by countries in the same region than by countries that are geographically dispersed. Moreover, lower transport costs — other things being equal — make the gains from trade greater for countries in the same region. Yet despite these incentives for regional groupings, FTAs are often not regional at all, but are formed for other reasons. An example was Commonwealth Preference, a "partial FTA" that reduced but did not eliminate tariffs among member countries with a common political tie.

not necessarily inferior for *each* of its members. [13] For example, one study calculates that, for Canada, an FTA with the United States may be superior to MFT. [14] The reason is that Canada will get a benefit from preference in the U.S. market in an FTA but not under MFT. This benefit could exceed Canada's FTA loss from trade diversion and from being unable to acquire the trade creation with third countries that would be available under MFT.

While countries can form an FTA while still working for MFT, the creation of an FTA may make it easier in some respects to negotiate MFT, and more difficult in others. Appendix 2-2 at the end of this chapter describes why.

Concluding Observations

By freeing trade between member countries, an FTA provides gains from trade based, for example, on comparative advantage, economies of scale, and increased competition in the domestic market of each participating country. In the absence of high costs from trade diversion, the net collective effect on member countries will, under standard assumptions, be positive. However, an FTA does have a protective effect against excluded countries, since discrimination is automatically created against their exports to FTA markets. This is true even in the type of FTA considered in this study — namely, an FTA in which member countries do not increase their trade barriers against excluded countries. However, if these trade barriers are increased when an FTA is formed, its protective effects that damage outsiders become even greater. Moreover, under standard assumptions, it also becomes less likely that the FTA will collectively benefit its members.

---

13 This conclusion is analogous to one that can be drawn for several regions within a country. Even in the typical case where retaining a national tariff is economically inferior to getting rid of it for all the nation's regions collectively, it is not necessarily inferior for *each* of its regions — or each of its "interest groups". Thus, even when a tariff is damaging to producers and consumers collectively, it will not necessarily be damaging to each group; in fact, it may well benefit producers.

14 David Cox and Richard G. Harris, "A Quantitative Assessment of the Economic Impact on Canada of Sectoral Free Trade with the United States," *Canadian Journal of Economics* 19 (August 1986): 386.

Appendix 2-1:
Trade Creation and Diversion in a Canadian-U.S. FTA, and in Its Extension to Include Mexico

The analysis so far suggests some of the reasons why both the Canada-U.S. FTA and its possible extension into a Canada-Mexico-U.S. FTA have been predicted, on balance, to be beneficial, even by those who have opposed other suggested FTAs. This box sets out these reasons. It is clearly not the full story, but it at least describes what the analysis in this chapter implies about these two FTAs.

The Canada-U.S. FTA

Harris and others have estimated that the Canada-U.S. FTA will generate net benefits.* The above discussion of trade creation and diversion provides some clues as to why. Broadly speaking, it is because the geographical proximity of the two countries means that they have an "economically natural" FTA — that is, their gains from trade are not dissipated in transport costs as they would be, for example, in a U.S.-Australia FTA. Because they trade more with each other than with anyone else, Canada and the United States are more likely to create, rather than divert, trade. For example, before the Canada-U.S. FTA, about 70 percent of Canadian imports were from the United States; this means that there has been only a small proportion of its import purchases (the remaining 30 percent) that Canada might divert from other countries to the United States. True, because U.S. trade is spread more evenly among countries, only about 20–25 percent of U.S. imports come from Canada, the largest U.S. trading partner. This means that there has been a larger

---

* For example, Cox and Harris estimate a 9 percent increase in Canadian welfare from bilateral free trade with the United States. See David Cox and Richard G. Harris, "A Quantitative Assessment of the Economic Impact on Canada of Sectoral Free Trade with the United States," *Canadian Journal of Economics* 19 (August 1986): 386. For reasons why the United States should also benefit (although by a smaller percentage), see Ronald J. Wonnacott and Paul Wonnacott, *Free Trade Between Canada and the United States: The Potential Economic Effects* (Cambridge, Mass.: Harvard University Press, 1967), p. 301.

proportion — about 75–80 percent — of its imports that the United States might divert from other countries to Canada. However, the cost to the United States of such diversion of its purchases to Canada may fall or disappear in some products because of the opportunities for falling costs in Canada based on economies of scale. Indeed, in some items Canadian costs may fall even further, thus allowing the United States to acquire these imports at lower cost than before the FTA.

A Broader North American FTA That Includes Mexico

The influences cited above in the Canada-U.S. FTA are likely to generate further trade creation benefits and limit any costs of trade diversion if that FTA is expanded to include Mexico. For example, Mexico is geographically proximate to the United States, with much of its trade centered there. Since about 70 percent of Mexican imports already come from the United States, there is limited scope for Mexican trade diversion. Thus, the proximity of the three countries and their existing trade patterns make it more likely that the benefits of trade creation will outweigh any net costs of diversion.

Appendix 2-2:
How the Creation of an FTA
May Affect the Prospects for MFT

An FTA May Make the
Negotiation of MFT More Difficult...

A standard objection to FTAs is that, by fragmenting the world's trading system into blocs of countries, they may weaken the prospects for MFT. Since countries in free trade blocs have already captured some of the benefits from free trade, they have less left to gain from a further move to MFT, and hence less incentive to pursue multilateral negotiations. In fact, it is possible that a country might resist MFT, because it would eliminate the FTA preference it gets in its partners' markets.

...Or Less Difficult

The reasons why an FTA may make it less difficult to negotiate MFT include the following:

•   By introducing more competition into the domestic markets of the member countries, an FTA may weaken special-interest groups in these countries, and thus reduce the resistance to any form of liberalization, including multilateral liberalization. Canada provides an example of how an FTA might make a member country more competitive and efficient. In the face of increased competition from the United States due to the Canada-U.S. FTA, there has been an effort in Canada to make the country more competitive by reducing interprovincial trade barriers. If this effort were to succeed in a significant way, Canada would be in a stronger position to engage in worldwide tariff reductions.

•   Because of the creation of an FTA, a member country may have an incentive to unilaterally cut its external tariffs against third countries, or let these tariffs decay. In other words, it may engage, on an *ad hoc* basis, in unilaterally liberalizing its trade with the rest of the world. Its objective may not be just to improve consumer welfare, but also to allow its firms to acquire the low-cost imported components from third countries that would put them in a stronger position to meet the new competition within the FTA. (Because this *ad hoc* liberalization makes it more difficult for its own manufacturers of these components to compete with third countries, there are two sides to this question, and often FTA members do not follow this policy.) The more that FTA members unilaterally lower their external tariffs, the less domestic resistance they will face in negotiating multilateral liberalization.

- A major FTA initiative may keep the process of trade liberalization going during a period in which the world would otherwise be slipping in the opposite direction toward increased protection. This is the "bicycle theory" of trade liberalization; if you do not somehow keep moving, you fall off.

- The gains from the creation of a large FTA may have a demonstration effect, making it clear to the rest of the world how beneficial trade liberalization can be. An FTA may "help provide the dynamism needed to make major improvements in the system and pave the way for broader multilateral agreements later on."[*]

- Some of the provisions negotiated for an FTA may provide a useful first draft for multilateral negotiations.

- An FTA may open up new areas of liberalization not previously addressed in multilateral negotiations. An example was the liberalized treatment of services negotiated in the Canada-U.S. FTA.

- The creation of an FTA may give excluded countries an incentive to work toward MFT as the only way of removing the discrimination the FTA imposes on them.

---

[*] Miriam Camps and William Diebold, Jr., *The New Multilateralism* (New York: Council on Foreign Relations, 1986), p. 68.

Chapter Three

The Economics of
Overlapping Free Trade Areas (I):
Toward a More General Theory
of Preferential Trading

The review of free trade areas (FTAs) in the previous chapter provides the basis for now examining how a hub-and-spoke regime would compare. Specifically, a hub-and-spoke system with a hub and two spokes (existing spoke *A* and new spoke *B*) will be compared in the next two chapters with a free trade area made up of exactly the same three countries.

While, for concreteness, readers may wish to think of the United States as the hub, Canada as existing spoke *A*, and Mexico as new spoke *B*, that example has not been used, except very rarely, in the next two chapters for two reasons. First, it is important to set out this analysis in general terms, since the hub-and-spoke problem applies not just to North America, but to any hemisphere or, for that matter, any set of countries. Second, the use of a North American example invites conclusions that are not justified until the empirical evidence on trade patterns has been examined (see Chapter 5).

How a Hub-and-Spoke System
Would Compare with a Free Trade Area

The Hub Country Would Benefit More
from a Hub-and-Spoke Than from an FTA

In a hub-and-spoke system, the benefits to the hub would be greater because it would get two advantages it would not under a tripartite FTA.

First, it would benefit in competition with the two spokes because only firms in the hub would be able to import inexpensive, duty-free inputs from both spokes.[1] Because of remaining trade barriers between the two spokes, firms in either spoke country would not be able to acquire duty-free inputs from the other.

Second, the hub would benefit from the preference it would get in the market of spoke *A* in competition with spoke *B*, and the preference it would get in the market of spoke *B* in competition with *A*.[2] The escalated nature of tariffs — that is, higher tariffs by each spoke on manufactures than on primary products — would strengthen the industrial preferences enjoyed by the hub.

In short, it would become easier for hub producers to compete with any spoke in the other spoke market for two reasons: (1) the costs of hub producers would be lower because they alone would be able to acquire low-priced inputs from both spokes; and (2) hub producers alone would get preferential duty-free access for their exports into both spoke markets. Both of these advantages for the hub arise because trade barriers between the spoke countries would *not* be eliminated. It is these barriers that would provide hub producers with a competitive advantage over firms in the spoke countries.

As the number of partners of the hub increases, the greater becomes the advantage for industry in the hub in acquiring inexpensive inputs from each spoke, and the larger becomes the number of spoke markets in which the hub would enjoy preference in competition with all other spoke countries. Thus, the preferential advantages to the hub country of a hub-and-spoke system over an FTA increases. Paradoxically, as the hub's partners increase, hub producers get preference (protection) in more and more foreign

---

1 The benefit to the hub will follow, assuming that these duty-free imports are not the result of trade diversion; or if they are, that the costs to the hub of its trade diversion are less than the benefits it receives. This assumption is made throughout the study.

2 The hub would, of course, get preference in each of these markets in competition with fourth countries as well. But since this is equally true in an FTA, it is not considered in this comparison of the two regimes. Nor are other common effects of an FTA and a hub-and-spoke considered. Another example might be an increase in U.S. protectionism triggered by duty-free imports from Mexico. For Canada, this could be a cost resulting from any form of Mexico-U.S. trade liberalization, whether in an FTA or a hub-and-spoke format.

markets, while they lose more and more of their protection in their own domestic market. The hub benefits from both of these changes, even though one increases the protection its producers receive while the other reduces it.[3]

This special preferential advantage to the hub becomes most pronounced in the hypothetical limit in which the hub has a spoke free trade bilateral with each of the other countries in the world. In that case, the alternative FTA, with all countries included, would, of course, become worldwide multilateral free trade (MFT). Under MFT, the hub would get no preference in any market, whereas under a worldwide hub-and-spoke system, the hub would get preference in *every* foreign market in competition with *all* other countries. The only market in which hub producers would not get preference (protection) over foreign firms would be the hub market itself. However, even in this market, as in all others, hub producers would enjoy a competitive advantage, since they alone would be able to acquire inexpensive imports from all other countries.

Trade Preferences Would Translate into a Location Advantage for the Hub

Because, in this worldwide hub-and-spoke system, the hub's producers alone would get duty-free inputs from all other countries, the entire hub country would get the industrial development advantage of becoming a duty-free, in-bond zone, with an additional advantage not available to such zones: preferential access to all export markets. It is easy to see in this context how a preferential trading system would translate into a locational advantage for investment in the hub country. Of course, in the more realistic case in which there were only a few spokes, the hub would get far less location advantage. It would be a duty-free zone only for imports from spoke countries, and it would get preference for its exports only

---

3 Under standard assumptions, reduced protection for its own producers in its own domestic market benefits the hub because its consumers/taxpayers get a net benefit that exceeds the loss to producers. On the other hand, increased protection in foreign markets provides the hub with a beneficial increase in the demand for its exports. (Much of the cost of this increased protection falls on the consumers in the *foreign* country where the protection is imposed.)

in spoke markets. However, this hypothetical example of a worldwide hub-and-spoke system does at least illustrate the trade and investment benefits the hub would be working toward if it were to extend its preferential trading system by adding more spokes.

Box 1 provides an example of the location advantages a country would receive if it were to become a hub.

Box 1: *Trade Preferences and Location Advantage:*
**   *The North American Case***

Before turning to the hub-and-spoke case, let me start with the simplest, most straightforward example of a two-country FTA: the present Canada-U.S. FTA. This tends to make the Canadian location more attractive because output produced there now has tariff-free access to the United States. It also tends to make the United States a more attractive location because of its tariff-free access to Canada.*

If this simple bilateral FTA is then extended into a U.S.-centered hub-and-spoke system by the creation of an overlapping bilateral — in this case, between Mexico and the United States — then this second bilateral will similarly create an attraction for foreign investment in Mexico and the United States. But this means that there would be a greater incentive for investment in the United States than in Canada or Mexico because the United States alone would be participating in both bilaterals. Production in the United States could be shipped duty free anywhere in Canada, Mexico, or the United States, whereas production in, say, Canada could be shipped duty free only throughout Canada and the United States. The particularly advantageous trade treatment that the U.S. hub would receive in alone getting preferential access to both spoke markets would increase the incentive for foreign firms — and U.S.-owned firms as well — to locate in the United States, rather than in Canada or Mexico. This attraction for investment in the United States would be augmented by the fact that the U.S. hub would be the only location in which firms could acquire duty-free imports from both Canada and Mexico.

To sum up, while investment in North America would still be influenced by a host of other factors, the trading preferences and lower input costs that the United States would enjoy in a hub-and-spoke system would translate into a substantial advantage in attracting investment.

* This does not guarantee that each will attract net investment, because each will have to compete with the other. But it does mean that both collectively will tend to attract investment from excluded countries.

Excluded Fourth Countries Would
Lose Less from a Hub-and-Spoke System

Excluded fourth countries would be damaged by either an FTA or a hub-and-spoke system, because either regime would leave them as outsiders facing discrimination in the markets of all three participating countries. Fourth countries would, however, incur less damage from a hub-and-spoke system, because the discrimination they would have to face in any spoke market would only be in competition with one country — the hub. In contrast, the discrimination they would have to face in an FTA would be in competition with *all* partners in the FTA.

The Hub's Partners
Would Prefer an FTA

The specific reasons why any of the hub's partners (say, country A) would prefer an FTA can be seen by considering the effects on A as a new partner B is added. In an FTA, country A would be likely to acquire net gains from free trade with B, due to (1) benefits from trade creation, including the acquisition of low-cost imports from B that would benefit A's consumers and make A's industry more competitive;[4] and (2) benefits to A's exporters of duty-free access to the market of B.

In comparison, under a hub-and-spoke system, A would fail to get free trade gains with the other spoke B, and would face two

---

4 Would A not divert more trade because there is a new partner B in the FTA? Not necessarily. True, A would engage in a new form of diversion as it switched some of its import purchases from excluded countries to B. On the other hand, A would eliminate the diversion of its import purchases from B to the higher-cost hub. It is difficult to assess how these two would compare.

In arguing that an expanding FTA would collectively benefit the participants, it is not necessary to assume that the costs of the new type of diversion would be offset by the benefits of eliminating the previous diversion. Instead, it is only necessary to make the much weaker and more realistic assumption that the costs of the new type of diversion would be more than offset by its benefits, plus the other benefits from an FTA — including the benefit from eliminating this previous diversion. This weaker assumption is implied in the rest of this study.

disadvantages that are the flip side of the preferential advantages the hub would get. First, *A* would be damaged by the discrimination it would have to face in *B*'s market in competition with the hub. (This is the flip side of the preferential benefit the hub would get in *B*'s market.) Second, *A* would suffer damage to its ability to compete with the hub's firms because they alone would get duty-free imports from other spoke *B*. Again, the flip side: industry in *A* would be at a competitive disadvantage precisely because industry in the hub would have a special advantage.

In short, country *A* should strongly prefer that a new free trade partner *B* be included in an expanded tripartite FTA, which would be likely to provide *A* with benefits from free trade with *B*, rather than have *B* sign another bilateral with the hub, which, by creating a hub-and-spoke regime, would impose discriminatory costs on *A*.[5]

Concluding Remarks: Lower Collective Income in a Hub-and-Spoke System

To sum up and extend this comparison of a hub-and-spoke and an FTA, a hub-and-spoke leaves barriers between the spoke countries, whereas an FTA does not. These barriers create beneficial preferences for the hub, but these same barriers are viewed by spoke countries as the costly discrimination they have to face. Moreover, these barriers mean that a hub-and-spoke system would, under standard assumptions, be less efficient and hence would generate

---

5 It is important to remember that, while an expanding hub-and-spoke system raises problems — and serious ones — for existing spoke country *A*, they are not as serious as the problems *A* would face if the hub were signing bilateral spoke agreements, *but none with A*. In that case, *A* would be an outsider right from the beginning. It would enjoy no initial benefits from a bilateral free trade agreement with the hub and it would simply be hammered by increasing levels of discrimination each time the hub were to add a new spoke — or, alternatively, if it were to expand a free trade area that continued to exclude *A*. Thus, this is *not* an argument that *A* should avoid an FTA with the hub in the first place. Rather, it is an argument that, once *A* has negotiated a bilateral free trade agreement with the hub, it is very much in *A*'s interest to have this expanded into a widening FTA, rather than a hub-and-spoke system.

less collective real income and growth than an FTA.[6] Therefore, the preferential benefits from a hub-and-spoke system that would go to the hub would be more than offset by discriminatory losses to its spoke partners. This provides the basis for the conclusion:

> *Compared with an FTA, the special benefits the hub re-*
> *ceives from the preferences it would get in a hub-and-spoke*
> *system could be expected to come completely at the ex-*
> *pense of its partner countries from the discrimination they*
> *would have to face; worse yet, these special preferences*
> *for the hub would generate a further deadweight loss.*

Now, let us turn from this comparison of a hub-and-spoke system with an FTA to the question: What happens if an FTA is not an option because the hub will offer only bilateral spoke agreements to new applicant countries?

What Happens as a Hub-and-Spoke System Develops: How It Compares with the Status Quo

The Hub Country Benefits

The hub would benefit from an expanding hub-and-spoke regime because it would get the benefits of free trade with all spoke countries, plus the special benefit of preference in each spoke market in competition with the other spoke countries.

Excluded Fourth Countries Would Lose

Any excluded country would lose because of the increasing number of spoke countries discriminating against it by giving preference to the hub. (True, an excluded country would lose less than it would

---

6 This is easiest to establish in the limiting case in which the hub has free trade with all other countries in the world. Then, an FTA becomes multilateral free trade, which, under standard assumptions, generates the highest attainable level of collective income. On the other hand, a hub-and-spoke, with its trade restraints between spoke countries left intact, leads to a different, less efficient outcome, and therefore a lower real income level. (For nonstandard assumptions that could upset this conclusion, see footnote 9 in Chapter 2.)

in the face of an expanding hemispheric FTA because the discrimination it would face would be less severe, but it would still lose.)

The Difficult Question: How Would Spoke Countries Be Affected?

Table 1 summarizes the reasons why a spoke country can expect to benefit from its own bilateral with the hub, but suffer losses from discrimination as the hub goes on to add new spokes.[7]

Effects on a Spoke When It Signs Its Own Bilateral with the Hub

Column 1 of Table 1 indicates that a spoke can expect to benefit when it signs its own bilateral free trade agreement with the hub because it will acquire not only the standard gains from trade creation based on economies of scale and comparative advantage, but also preference in the hub market, because the agreement is for a limited bilateral FTA rather than multilateral free trade. Of course, the limited preferential nature of the agreement means that the spoke country will also divert some trade, which will involve a terms-of-trade loss along with benefits from increased production and consumption efficiency. Since it is not clear how these positive and negative effects will compare, the net effect of diversion could be positive or negative. However, even if it is negative, the overall net effect on the spoke from its bilateral with the hub (the combined effects in column 1) will still be positive, in the absence of the following unlikely set of circumstances: (1) the net effect of trade diversion is negative, with terms-of-trade losses exceeding efficiency

---

7 There are two reasons why, in the analysis of this chapter, the addition of new spokes has such a negative effect on an existing spoke. First, it is assumed that each spoke's trade with the hub is competitive rather than complementary; thus, for example, increased U.S. imports from Mexico will, other things being equal, reduce rather than increase U.S. demand for imports from Canada. Second, the analysis concentrates on the direct effects of trade preferences — or, from the existing spoke's point of view, trade discrimination. It does not take into account, for example, the indirect spillover benefits to the existing spoke of increased income in the new spokes. This is one of the issues discussed in the next chapter. (Indirect spillover benefits may also go to excluded fourth countries, reducing their losses.)

**Table 1:   *The Economics of Preferential Trading:
The Effects on a Spoke as a Hub-and-
Spoke System Develops***

Expected Effects on a Spoke from Its Own Bilateral with the Hub	Expected Effects on the Existing Spoke Each Time the Hub Adds a New Spoke	
	"Free trade" effect — that is, the effect on existing spoke A that occurs because the hub gets free trade with new spoke B. This effect on existing spoke A occurs whether the negotiations between the hub and new spoke B are bilateral or trilateral (including A).	*"Protective" effects — that is, the effects of the protection that remains between existing spoke A and new spoke B. These effects on spoke A occur because the agreement between the hub and new spoke B is bilateral and excludes the existing spoke. These effects would not occur in an expanding trilateral FTA.*
(1)	*(2)*	*(3)*
Gains from free trade, augmented by two "bilateral" effects that occur because the agreement is with the hub only:	Loss to existing spoke A from the elimination of its preference over new spoke B in the hub's market.	Damage to existing spoke A from the discrimination it now has to face in the market of new spoke B.
(a) the benefit of preference acquired in the hub's market; and		Reduced ability of spoke A's firms to compete with the hub's firms in the hub's market (and in other markets as well) because only the hub's firms get duty-free inputs from all spokes.
(b) the effect of trade diversion[a]		
Likely net effect:		
Positive	Negative	Negative

[a] The net effect of trade diversion could be positive or negative, since the definition used here includes both unfavorable terms-of-trade effects and favorable effects on production and consumption efficiency from reducing domestic price toward the world level.

gains; *and* (2) it is sufficiently negative to offset the other benefits in column 1.

The next question is: What happens to a spoke country when the hub then proceeds to add a new spoke?

Effects on an Existing Spoke
When the Hub Adds a New Spoke

There are two sets of effects, set out in columns 2 and 3 in Table 1. The "free trade" effect on the existing spoke shown in column 2 arises because the hub and new spoke are *liberalizing their trade*. This effect on the existing spoke will occur whether this trade liberalization is in a hub-and-spoke configuration or in an expanding FTA. The "protective" effects in column 3 arise *only* in a hub-and-spoke configuration because of the protection it leaves between spokes — protection that would not exist in an expanding FTA. Consider each in turn.

The free trade effect (column 2). To illustrate, suppose the U.S. hub were to add a new spoke bilateral with Mexico to go along with its existing spoke bilateral with Canada. Because Mexico would now have duty-free access to the U.S. hub, the preference in the U.S. market over Mexico that existing spoke Canada negotiated in its own earlier bilateral with the U.S. hub would disappear. This would be a limited loss for Canada, since it would still retain the preference it negotiated in the U.S. hub over other countries. It is a loss nonetheless.

It should be re-emphasized that this effect on the existing spoke will occur once the hub and the new spoke decide to liberalize their trade, whether it be in a bilateral hub-and-spoke or trilateral FTA format. Thus, the existing spoke cannot, by participating in tri-lateralizing the negotiations, protect itself from this loss of part of the privilege it negotiated in its bilateral with the hub. There may be other respects in which the existing spoke can protect itself by participating in the negotiations, but this is not one.

"Protective" effects on the existing spoke because it is excluded from the hub's bilateral free trade agreement with the new spoke (col-umn 3). The two protective effects in column 3 arise solely because

the system is developing not as a trilateral FTA, but in a hub-and-spoke configuration that leaves protection between spoke countries intact. They are, of course, the two reasons identified earlier in our comparison of an FTA and a hub-and-spoke system that explain why an existing spoke will prefer an FTA. The first is the discrimination the existing spoke has to face in the market of the new spoke. The second is the competitive disadvantage of producers in the existing spoke because they cannot acquire duty-free inputs from the new spoke.

The Economics of Preferential Trading: The Summary Effects on a Spoke Country as a Hub-and-Spoke System Develops

The following two broad effects on a spoke country have been identified in Table 1. First, the spoke can expect to benefit from its own bilateral with the hub (column 1) — especially if the hub is relatively large. Second, in columns 2 and 3, it can expect to incur costs as the hub goes on to sign further bilaterals with new spokes.[8]

What Defense Do Spoke Countries Have?

Why would an existing spoke country not avoid the two costs of trade distortions in column 3 by removing its own tariff? The answer is that this would only allow it to escape from the second of these costs, by providing its industry with duty-free inputs from the other spoke. But it would not allow it to avoid the other cost, since it would still have to face discrimination in the other spoke's market.

But since removing its own tariff is in the interests of each spoke country, why would they not all do it? By eliminating all protection between spokes, this would apparently also allow each of the spokes to avoid the other cost in column 3, since there would no longer be discrimination among spokes. In effect, such unilateral

---

8 Of course, for the last spoke included, benefits from its own bilateral with the hub follows, rather than precedes, the accumulation of costs. However, the conclusion still holds for this spoke, as indeed it does, subject to a similar caveat, for all other spokes in the sequence.

action independently taken by all spokes would seem to transform a hub-and-spoke system into an FTA. Why would this not just happen through independent unilateral action by a group of countries, each following its own economic interest?

One reason is that such unilateral action by the spokes cannot completely succeed in transforming the system into an FTA, for esoteric reasons described in Box 2 that have to do with rules of origin. A second reason is a political one: one cannot expect spoke countries to cut their tariffs unilaterally, for the same reasons that countries have not unilaterally removed their tariffs in the past and thus created world free trade, even though it may have been in the individual interest of each to do so. These reasons include the political difficulties faced by any government in selling a policy of "making concessions" (removing its own tariffs) without requiring the same concessions from its trading partners; the further political difficulties generated by the resistance of import-competing special-interest groups that oppose removal of their own protection when the government cannot call on export industries to give it the necessary offsetting support (as it can in a reciprocal negotiation); and the relatively high short-run adjustment costs of a policy that reduces employment in import-competing sectors without offering obvious employment increases in export sectors.[9]

Why Would Countries Be Willing to Become New Spokes?

Even though a prospective new partner would, like an existing partner, prefer an FTA to a hub-and-spoke regime, it may still have an incentive to say yes to a spoke bilateral if that is all it is offered — that is, if joining an FTA is not an option.

Why might a country be willing to do this, and thus participate in an inferior, discriminatory, and perhaps ultimately damaging

---

9 Employment increases would indeed occur, but in a more subtle way. The exchange-rate decrease expected to follow from unilateral tariff reductions would, *ceteris paribus*, increase export employment and reduce the pressure on import-competing sectors. But this is difficult for the public to understand, especially since, in many other contexts, a falling value of an exchange rate may be an indication of policy failure.

Box 2: *Transforming a Hub-and-Spoke System into a FTA: The Rules-of-Origin Problem*

To illustrate the importance of rules of origin, suppose there is a Canada-Mexico-U.S. FTA with a 50 percent rule of origin. A good with 25 percent U.S. content, 25 percent Mexican content, and zero Canadian content would enter Canada from Mexico duty free. But this good would not enter Canada from Mexico duty free if there were instead a hub-and-spoke system and Canada were unilaterally to eliminate its tariffs against Mexico, subject to the same 50 percent rule of origin; obviously this good could not enter Canada duty free, since it would only have 25 percent Mexican content.

Moreover, this problem cannot be resolved by a unilateral redefinition of rules of origin by Canada and by Mexico. To create an FTA in this way requires the U.S. hub to redefine its rules of origin as well (as detailed in footnote 1 on p. 71). Furthermore, each unilateral removal by a spoke of its tariffs against other spokes would violate the "most-favored-nation" requirement in Article 1.1 of the General Agreement on Tariffs and Trade because this concession would be provided only to other spokes rather than to all countries.

But would these problems not be avoided and the system transformed into an FTA if each spoke were to eliminate its tariffs unilaterally not just against other spokes, but against all countries (with no rules of origin then required)? The reasons why governments resist any such politically controversial policy are discussed in the text. But even if such a policy were politically feasible, it would not yield the same outcome as an FTA, since spokes would have removed their tariffs not only against each other, but also against all outside fourth countries. Moreover, the U.S. hub would likely object to this, since it would damage U.S. firms (and according to footnote 5 in Chapter 2, the U.S. economy as well) by removing the preference the United States previously negotiated in each spoke market, not only against other spokes, but also against outside fourth countries.

Thus, no matter which of these two unilateral routes the spokes might take, the U.S. hub would in some way become involved. Therefore, the transformation of a hub-and-spoke system into an FTA would require a trilateral negotiation by all three participants with the best, but far from guaranteed, possible outcome being the trilateral FTA they could have negotiated in the first place.

trading regime? One answer is that it may be short-sighted, seeing only the immediate benefit of joining (free access to the hub's market), but not the subsequent buildup of costs as the hub goes on to add other spokes. This, however, is not the fundamental reason, since it will still have an incentive to join, even were it to have perfect foresight and fully recognize the accumulating costs. Indeed, it will still have an incentive to say yes even if it can perfectly foresee that it is joining a hub-and-spoke process that will eventually make it, on balance, *worse off.* The reason for this is that all the new spoke's answer will do is give it the benefits of free trade with the hub. If it says yes, it gets them; if it says no, it does not. Its decision has little influence over the hub as it adds spokes, allowing the trading system to be carved into a preferential network. That will or will not happen regardless; it is a cost the prospective new spoke will have to face whether or not it decides to join the hub-and-spoke system. The only decision for that country is for free trade with the hub or not, and the answer to that — in terms of the economic issues discussed here — is likely to be yes, especially if the hub is a large and wealthy country. The new spoke may resent the whole process — and, in particular, the dominant role the hub plays in damaging its trade prospects down the road — but it will still be in its economic interests to say yes.

Thus, if the hub were to judge a hub-and-spoke system to be its own best option for reasons cited so far — a view that will, in the light of broader considerations, be seriously questioned later — it would be very easy for the hub to see such a development take place. All it has to do is offer only spoke bilaterals, and it is unlikely to run out of new applicants. Moreover, the more spokes the hub already has, the greater will be the incentive for new countries to participate. Consider a hypothetical situation facing country *V*, the last holdout in a hub-and-spoke world. From *V*'s point of view, the hub has completed the carving-up process, which by now has left *V* facing the maximum amount of discrimination it can ever face. It has already borne all the costs of the hub-and-spoke system. *V*'s decision on becoming the last spoke by getting a bilateral with the hub is therefore a clean one. Saying yes involves only the net benefit of free trade with the hub, but no costs down the road. The question for *V* is: Now that its trading prospects have been damaged, does it want to recoup by cashing in a benefit?

Beyond this analysis, there may be a further incentive for a country to say yes if it is offered a spoke bilateral and views it as the only way of liberalizing its trade with a large and wealthy hub with which it already trades heavily. The prospective spoke may view such a bilateral as the only way to reduce the risks that its existing exports will be subject to protective action by the hub. For example, Mexico has viewed a bilateral free trade agreement with the United States as a way of reducing the risk of being the target of "Super-301" or some other form of U.S. unilateral action. Thus, like Canada in the last decade, its objective may not be just to get better access to the U.S. market, but also to reduce the risk of having its existing access damaged by unilateral U.S. action. This raises a question. Could aggressive U.S. *unilateral* policies, such as Super-301, that were developed during the 1980s be used in the 1990s in a way in which they were not originally intended: to put pressure on U.S. trading partners to participate in a new U.S. *bilateralism* — specifically, in the development of a U.S.-centered hub-and-spoke system? In my judgment, this is not why these unilateral U.S. policies were introduced; nonetheless, they might end up being used in this way, either by inadvertence or design.

Concluding Remarks

This completes the discussion of the economics of preferential trading, beginning with the traditional economics of simple free trade areas in Chapter 2, and then in Chapter 3 covering the more complex economics of overlapping free trade areas — that is, hub-and-spoke systems. The development of a such a system will generate special preferential benefits for the hub country and losses to excluded outside countries. For a spoke country, it is not clear how the benefits from its own bilateral with the hub may compare with the discrimination and other disadvantages it has to face as the hub country goes on to add new spokes. The central conclusion, however, *is* clear: spoke countries will view a hub-and-spoke system as inferior to joining an expanding FTA.

Chapter Four

The Economics of
Overlapping Free Trade Areas (II):
Extending the Analysis
beyond Preferential Trading

The analysis in Chapter 3 concentrated entirely on the effects of preferential trading and led to the conclusion that a hub-and-spoke system would be in the interest of the hub, whereas a free trade area (FTA) would be in the interests of the spokes. But this is too simple. In this chapter, some other expected effects of a hub-and-spoke system are examined. It turns out that each of these effects represents a disadvantage of a hub-and-spoke system — compared with an FTA — for all participating countries, spokes and hub alike. Thus, these are additional reasons for each spoke to prefer an FTA, and may be reasons for the hub to reverse its assessment and also prefer an FTA.

The Indirect Spillover Effect
of Growth in Each New Spoke

Free trade with the hub can be expected to increase income substantially in a new spoke, especially if the hub is large and wealthy — for example, the European Community in Europe, the United States in the Americas, or Japan in East Asia. In all these cases, it is easy to identify potential spokes whose income could double, or triple, or more. With the new spoke's income rising, the hub and all existing spokes can expect a spillover benefit in the form of increased exports.

The first important conclusion is that it is no longer so clear that once a spoke has benefited from its own bilateral with the hub it will then lose as the hub goes on to add a new spoke. That will depend on whether or not the increased discrimination the existing spoke has to face will be offset by the spillover benefits it will realize from growth in the new spoke.

There is another important conclusion: Whatever the expected increase in income in the new spoke may be, it will be greater if it is joining an expanding FTA instead — since it will be trading freely not just with the hub, but with all its FTA partners. Consequently, existing spokes and the hub will find the spillover benefit from growth in the new spoke greater in an FTA than in a hub-and-spoke system. This, then, is one reason for all participating countries to prefer an FTA.

The Waste of Real Resources in a Hub-and-Spoke System Due to Higher Administrative and Transport Costs

Suppose, for the moment, that a hub-and-spoke system has developed in which the U.S. hub has consistent — indeed, identical — bilaterals with all of the spokes. (Such consistency has been implicitly assumed so far.) Because this would be a more complex trading network than an FTA, there would be a waste of the extra time and effort that management, economists, lawyers, and accountants would have to devote to determining the least expensive trade and investment patterns throughout this maze.

To illustrate, it would become profitable to redirect some Mexican-Canadian trade into a duty-free route through the U.S. hub. True, if a hub-and-spoke system were extended throughout South America, it is unlikely that Argentine-Brazilian trade would be similarly routed through the United States, since, in this case, higher transport costs would almost certainly more than offset any tariff savings from the duty-free U.S. route. Nonetheless, there are many intermediate cases. For example, should some Brazil-Canada trade be redirected through the duty-free United States? While the extra time and effort that would go into answering such questions would provide a private payoff to lawyers, economists, accountants, and the trading firms hiring them, from a broader point of view it would be an unnecessary waste of these resources.

This waste of resources in extra administrative costs in a hub-and-spoke system would go hand in hand with a similar waste due to the higher transport costs incurred in rerouting trade. It should be emphasized that such extra administrative and transport costs — with the waste in resources these imply — would be above the waste and inefficiency that would occur even in a hub-and-spoke system in which such costs did not exist — in other words, above and beyond the inefficiencies in the hub-and-spoke system described in Chapter 3.

The Problem of Rent Seeking in a Hub-and-Spoke System

As a hub-and-spoke system develops, the question arises: Which country will be next? Then there is the possibility of lobbying pressure by rent-seeking firms in the hub to influence the selection of the country or a sequence of countries that will provide these firms with special preferential benefits. The argument here is parallel to the traditional one in which rent-seeking firms seek to establish special benefits from the creation of, say, a monopoly position. Both preference in a foreign market and a domestic monopoly position are created by restricting the entry of competitors; in the case of trade preference described here, it is the entry of spoke competitors into other spoke markets that is restricted. In either case, rent seeking represents a social waste, though, of course, it may provide a benefit to the firms that engage in this activity.[1] Moreover, it would not be limited to firms in the hub; firms in spoke countries and prospective spoke countries may also engage in rent-seeking attempts to influence the sequencing of bilaterals.

These rent-seeking wastes will escalate if it is no longer assumed that all bilaterals are consistent.

Rent-Seeking Waste in an Inconsistent *Hub-and-Spoke System*

For good reasons — such as the desire by each spoke country to negotiate an agreement tailored to its own special needs — the

---

1 In an expanding FTA, there may also be rent-seeking attempts to influence the sequence of new partners. But these attempts are likely to be less wasteful, because an FTA is a less complex trading arrangement, with fewer trade constraints restricting the entry of competitors.

bilaterals in a hub-and-spoke system are unlikely to be consistent. The result will be an increased incentive for rent seeking, with the waste this implies. Thus, tailoring may become both a motive for a country to seek a bilateral and a cause of wasted resources because of the efforts of rent-seeking firms.

Other Kinds of Waste in an Inconsistent Hub-and-Spoke System

Inconsistency of the bilaterals will increase two other costs described above. First, transport costs are likely to increase as the network becomes more inconsistent and complex. Second, the administrative waste of legal, accounting, and other resources devoted to defining the best routing of trade and location of production will increase (see Box 3).

The Problem of Managed Trade

Negotiators may have an incentive to include elements of managed trade in any FTA, since this allows them to solve two problems at once: (1) the free trade provisions increase efficiency and generate support from free traders, while (2) the managed trade provisions, with their cartel-like, market-sharing provisions, protect employment and generate support from protectionists.

Is a bilateral agreement more or less likely than an expanding FTA to include elements of managed trade? There is no clear theoretical answer to this question. It is possible for a spoke bilateral to include more free trade provisions than could be achieved in a plurilateral expansion of an FTA. Indeed, one of the traditionally cited advantages of a bilateral over a multilateral negotiation is that greater progress in liberalizing trade may be possible for two countries than for more than that number. This could similarly be an advantage of a bilateral over a plurilateral expansion of an FTA. However, the problem is that it is also possible in a bilateral for the two countries to negotiate *less* free trade by cartelizing markets in managed trade configurations.

This, then, is a caution and warning, rather than a prediction of what will happen: Because only two countries are participating

Box 3: *Waste in an Inconsistent*
Set of Bilateral Trade Agreements

A hypothetical example of the waste, confusion, and complexity in an inconsistent set of bilateral trade agreements was provided by Derek H. Burney, Canadian Ambassador to the United States, in an address to the University of Texas at Austin on March 6, 1991:

> Imagine the difficulty that, say, a Texas entrepreneur would face in conducting an export business. Would the entrepreneur be comfortable with three, or five, or ten distinct trade agreements, each with its own documents, definitions, and regulations? What a bonanza for lawyers and trade consultants!
>
> There would be more practical handicaps too.
>
> Let us say that a business firm here in Texas seeks to use its own technology to manufacture left-handed widget components in Chile, have them assembled in Mexico, incorporate them into ambidextrous widgets in Canada and export the new product for sale in the United States.
>
> Separate agreements may cause impossible complications.
>
> For example, Chile may not protect the technology in question. Certain copyright laws have not been built into their bilateral agreement.
>
> Mexico's duty on widget components has not been eliminated. Sorry, that bilateral agreement has a special protective provision for widget assembly permitting only national components.
>
> Canada, for its part, can use only a minimum amount of non-Canadian content in widgets exported to the United States. Pity, but this provision was imposed by the U.S. Congress on the U.S.-Canada Free Trade Agreement to ensure that the northern neighbor did not become a back door into the United States for foreign-made components.
>
> These are some of the troubles which separate agreements, separately arrived at, can make for American, Canadian, or Mexican exporters.

in the negotiation of a spoke bilateral, there is a risk that it will be tailored to include more managed trade than would occur in the expansion of an FTA. Note that the same risk arises in trade negotiations covering single industries. In either case, the fewer the players, the easier it may be for cartel-like arrangements to be set up by negotiators who, recognizing the political resistance to their trade agreement that must be overcome, may have an incentive to neutralize some opposition groups by providing them with managed trade provisions.

But why is managed trade inferior to free trade? While managed trade protects existing producer interests, and thus generates less short-run adjustment cost, in the long run it is not as efficient as unmanaged free trade. Under standard assumptions, the higher, less competitive prices typically associated with managed trade imply losses to the consuming public that exceed the benefits to existing producers; moreover, because these producers are "protected" by managed trade provisions, they may become less able to meet foreign competition. Indeed, the whole process of reallocating resources between industries in order to capture benefits from comparative advantage and economies of scale will be deterred by a managed trade insulation of existing producer interests.

The Cure for Poverty
in the Americas: Trade, Not Aid

The traditional list of advantages of trade over aid to cure poverty need not be repeated here in detail. Suffice it to note that trade is preferred by the higher-income country because it receives goods and services in return if it trades, but not if it grants aid. Moreover, trade is preferred by the lower-income country because it is never placed in a supplicant status; instead, it solves its problems through its own efforts. Finally, both countries have an interest in trade because it avoids the hostility that the recipient of aid may develop against the donor.

By opening access for Latin American countries into the U.S. market, either a hub-and-spoke or an expanded FTA will provide the benefits of trade rather than aid. However, an expanding FTA will provide more of these benefits, not only because low-income countries in the Americas will get free access to the high-income Canadian market as well, but also because they will get free access to each others' markets. This will provide them not only with economic benefits but also with the assurance that they are participating together in a common effort to raise income.

Concluding Remarks

The problems described in this chapter represent reasons why a hub-and-spoke system is less efficient than an FTA and would lead to a lower collective real income level. All of these depressing effects on efficiency and income are in addition to those that would exist in a hub-and-spoke system even in the world of Chapter 3, where there were no transport or administrative costs, rent-seeking waste, or any inconsistencies whatsoever in the spoke bilaterals. Recognition of these problems leads to an even less favorable assessment of a hub-and-spoke system by all countries. The conclusion so far is that a hub-and-spoke system is even worse for the spoke countries than the theory of preferential trading indicated. Moreover, it can no longer be convincingly argued that, in comparison to an FTA, there would be an overall net benefit even for the hub, the beneficiary of the special preferences in a hub-and-spoke system.

Chapter Five

Trade Patterns in the Americas:
Background for the
Mexican Free Trade Decision

With this theoretical discussion of the two trade regimes now complete, it is appropriate to turn to the evidence on trading patterns in the Americas. What do these patterns reveal about whether Mexican free trade should be in the form of a trilateralization of the Canada-U.S. Free Trade Agreement (FTA) or a Mexico-U.S. spoke bilateral? Does this question matter at all, since the only *prima facie* difference between the two regimes is whether or not Mexico and Canada will be trading freely, and there is now a relatively small trade flow between them?

Surprises in a
Hemisphere of Unbalanced Trade

The first surprise is the degree to which trade in the whole Western Hemisphere is concentrated in North America. The three bilateral trade relationships between the United States, Canada, and Mexico cover over $225 billion of trade. (All figures are for 1989 in US$ billions.) Compare this with the $15 billion of trade covered by the ten bilateral trade relationships between the five largest trading nations in Central and South America — Argentina, Brazil, Chile, Colombia, and Venezuela. Largely because of Canada-U.S. trade — the *world's* largest trading relationship — the picture in the hemisphere is one of a North American trading powerhouse in which Mexico also plays an important role. In contrast, there is relatively little trading activity to the south.

While it is not surprising that the United States, with its large export capacity and demand for imports, would be the dominant trader in the hemisphere, the degree to which this is true still does come as a surprise. Indeed, the United States is the most important partner for almost every substantial trading country in the Americas. Even Argentina, which has $1.8 billion of two-way trade with nearby Brazil, has more trade ($2.5 billion) with the distant United States. For Brazil, the dominance of the United States is even stronger. Its two-way trade with the distant United States is $13.8 billion, compared with its $1.8 billion of trade with adjacent Argentina.

The third surprise is how small two-way trade is between Mexico and Canada ($2.1 billion), even though both have a large trading relationship with the United States. Canada's trade with Mexico is only slightly more than 1 percent of its trade with the United States.[1] Nonetheless, that small Canada-Mexico trade is still the hemisphere's largest bilateral relationship, excluding those in which the United States participates.

These observations provide a background for a more detailed display of trading patterns.

Trade Patterns in Detail

Exports and Imports in the Americas

Table 2 shows 1989 exports and imports of selected countries in the hemisphere with each other. In the northwest corner of the table, the dominance of the Canada-U.S. relationship is confirmed, with Mexico-U.S. also important. A move away from this corner shows how quickly other bilateral trade relationships fade in comparison. For example, note the almost miniscule trade between two important countries, Mexico and Venezuela. (Part of the reason is that an important export of each is oil, and that is not conducive to trade between the two.)

Table 3 reproduces the exports and imports of the United States and its four largest trading partners in the Western Hemisphere, and shows the trade of each of them with all Latin American countries except Cuba. To put this in global perspective, note that,

---

1 Official figures on Canada-Mexico trade are undoubtedly biased downward, insofar as some of this trade passes through the United States and is not recorded as being between Mexico and Canada.

Table 2: **Trade Among Selected Countries of the Western Hemisphere, 1989**
(US$ billions)

Exporting Country ↓ \ Importing Country →	United States	Canada	Mexico	Brazil	Venezuela	Colombia	Argentina	Chile	Ecuador	Panama	Bolivia	Peru	Uruguay	Jamaica	Costa Rica	Total (world)
United States		82.0	25.0	4.8	3.0	1.9	1.0	1.4	0.6	0.7	0.1	0.7	0.1	1.0	0.9	369.0
Canada	89.6		0.5	0.5	0.1	0.2		0.1	0.1	0.1		0.1		0.1	0.1	121.0
Mexico	27.6	1.6							0.2	0.1				0.1	0.1	37.1
Brazil	9.0	1.1	0.4		0.3	0.2	0.7	0.7			0.2	0.1	0.3			33.0
Venezuela	7.2	0.6				0.3		0.2						0.1		12.0
Colombia	2.7	0.2		0.2	0.3		0.1	0.1	0.1			0.1				5.7
Argentina	1.5	0.1	0.2	1.1		0.1		0.4			0.1	0.2	0.2			10.0
Chile	1.5	0.2		0.4		0.1	0.1				0.1	0.1				8.2
Ecuador	1.6	0.2				0.1		0.1				0.1				2.4
Panama	0.3															0.3
Bolivia	0.1															0.8
Peru	0.9	0.1		0.1	0.1	0.1		0.1								3.5
Uruguay	0.2	0.1		0.4												1.6
Jamaica	0.6	0.2														1.0
Costa Rica	1.1	0.1							0.1							1.5
Total (world)	493.0	129.0	33.7	20.0	7.6	5.0	4.2	6.5	1.9	1.0	0.8	2.1	1.2	1.8	1.8	

Note: All data are import figures except for the last column and U.S. and Canadian exports to Latin America. In a few cases, inconsistencies in the data — for example, between the export figure of one country and the corresponding import figure of its trading partner — have had to be arbitrarily resolved. Thus, beyond those for Canada and the United States, these data do not have a high degree of accuracy. Since the data have been rounded to the nearest $100 million, any trade flow of less than $50 million does not appear.

Source: International Monetary Fund, *Direction of Trade Statistics, 1991* (Washington, D.C., 1991).

very broadly speaking, these figures are in roughly the same ball-
park as the trade of these five countries with Japan, with deviations
from this pattern as expected — that is, Brazil and Venezuela,
located within Latin America, trade more with that area than with
Japan, while Canada, located at a distance from Latin America,
trades more with Japan.

In Figure 2, panel (a) shows the United States' two-way trade
with its four largest trading partners in the Americas and indicates
how U.S. hemispheric trade is dominated by the Canadian relationship, with Mexico an important second, and others tailing off.

Panel (b) shows an even stronger conclusion for Canada. Its
trade with the United States overwhelms its trade with any Latin
American country. Panel (c) indicates that the same is true of
Mexico, even though it is itself a Latin American country.

The Implications of Existing Trade Patterns

These figures yield six conclusions that are important in comparing
a hub-and-spoke system with an expanding free trade area in the
specific context of North America and, more broadly, the Western
Hemisphere.

*1. The United States has an even more dominant
trading position than is often supposed.*

This raises an important question to be addressed in the next
chapter: Would an FTA or a hub-and-spoke system increase this
U.S. dominance?

*2. The main interest of most countries in the Western
Hemisphere is in free trade with the United States,
since the United States is their largest trading partner and is also technologically their most challeng-
ing partner.*

The GNP data in Figure 3 suggest that free trade with the United
States may well bring large percentage gains in productivity and
income to Mexico and other Latin American countries — indeed,

Table 3: **Trade Among the United States and Its Four Largest Western Hemispheric Trading Partners, Plus Japan, 1989**

(US$ billions)

Exporting Country ↓ / Importing Country →	United States	Canada	Mexico	Brazil	Venezuela	All Latin America (except Cuba)	Japan
United States		82.0	25.0	4.8	3.0	49.1	44.6
Canada	89.6		0.5	0.5	0.1	2.0	7.4
Mexico	27.6	1.6		0.2	0.1	1.3	1.7
Brazil	9.0	1.1	0.4		0.3	3.9	3.0
Venezuela	7.2	0.6		0.2		2.7	0.5
All Latin America (except Cuba)	60.1	4.5	1.2	3.7	0.9		8.5
Japan	97.1	8.9	1.4	1.3	0.3	8.8	

Note: All data are for imports, except for U.S. and Canadian exports to Latin America and the last two columns.

Source: International Monetary Fund, *Direction of Trade Statistics, 1991* (Washington, D.C., 1991).

Figure 2:   *Two-Way Trade, 1989*
(US$ billions)

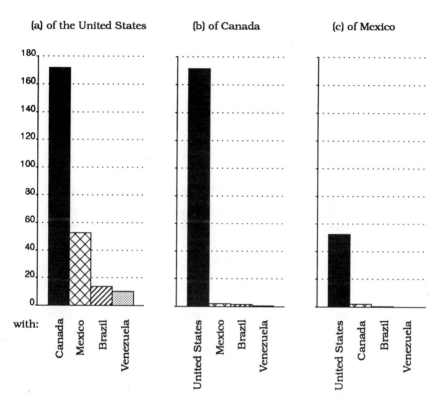

Source: International Monetary Fund, *Direction of Trade Statistics, 1991* (Washington, D.C., 1991).

much larger gains than can be expected for Canada from its free trade with the United States. This is because productivity and income in a country such as Mexico are now so low. Income per capita in Mexico is roughly 10 percent of the U.S. level, while Mexican productivity is little better.[2] If free trade with the United

---

2 Preliminary results from a current study by Clark Reynolds at Stanford University comparing employed workers in the two countries indicate that Mexican productivity may be about 20 percent of the U.S. level, with per capita GNP lower because of a lower participation rate. (This 20 percent figure will overstate to the degree that the lower participation rate itself is just another manifestation of low Mexican productivity.)

Figure 3: *Gross National Product Per Capita, Selected Countries*

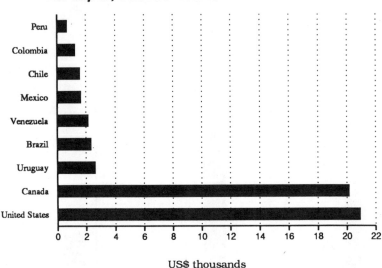

US$ thousands

Note: These data are sensitive to changes in exchange rates. All are 1989 data except for Brazil and Colombia (1988), Mexico (1987), and Peru (1985).

Source: International Monetary Fund, *International Financial Statistics* (February 1991).

States were to cut this productivity gap by a third or even a quarter, Mexican productivity and income could double or more — a three-digit percentage increase. Compare this with the case of Canada, where the largest estimated gain in productivity and income from free trade with the United States is in the single-digit range.

There are a number of reasons to expect that, over the short term, free trade would partially, but far from completely, close this productivity gap for a country such as Mexico. A substantial increase in Mexican productivity should be possible as multinationals combine more capital with Mexican labor and organize that labor more efficiently. However, it will take longer to raise Mexican productivity by putting in place the necessary industrial infrastructure, such as adequate transport and telecommunications systems. It will take longer yet to raise Mexican productivity through improvements in education.

Nonetheless, for a country such as Mexico, a large increase in income is still possible even in the short term from a very limited closure of its productivity gap with the United States. This strengthens the expectation that, even in a hub-and-spoke system, Mexico would get a large benefit from its own initial free trade with the United States. Moreover, it makes it less clear that Mexico and Canada would be damaged if the United States were to go on to add further new spokes in Latin America. The reason is that these other Latin American countries are like Mexico: they also have large productivity and income gaps with the United States and may accordingly acquire large income gains from free trade with the United States. Such gains could be expected to have large spillover effects in increasing the demand for Mexican and Canadian goods.

On the other hand, the evidence suggests one reason why spoke Mexico — or for that matter, Canada — might suffer *greater* damage if the United States were to continue to add new spokes in Central and South America. The small trade between the United States and almost all of the Central and South American countries suggests that they might, in practice, find themselves in the "Israeli" position of selling an insufficient quantity of exports to the United States to do enough damage to trigger U.S. trade remedy action. They may thus be able to get better access to the U.S. market than Canadian or Mexican exporters, who would face a continued risk of such U.S. action and hence would find it more difficult to compete.

3. Mexican trade diversion in a hub-and-spoke system would cause little damage to existing Canadian exports, but could substantially damage future Canadian exports.

To clarify this conclusion, note that, with 1989 Canadian exports to Mexico running at only $0.5 billion, there are simply too few present Mexican purchases from Canada to make a trade-diverting switch by Mexico to U.S. sources of supply very damaging. To put this another way, there will be little diversion of present Mexican trade away from Canada since there is very little of this trade to divert. The importance of this Mexican diversion, however, may increase in the future — indeed, the expectation of a large Mexican income gain suggests a growing potential for increased future trade between Canada and Mexico. In this event, some Mexican trade with Canada that would have otherwise developed in an expanded FTA might instead, because of the hub-and-spoke discrimination Canada would face in the Mexican market, never come to exist. Instead, it would be "diverted" to the United States. In short, the disadvantage of a hub-and-spoke system is not so much that *present* Canadian exports to Mexico would be diverted as that *future* Canadian exports would be, and hence would never come to exist at all.

This section has considered the damage to Canada of hub-and-spoke restrictions on its exports to Mexico. Now we turn to the damage to Canada from restrictions on its *imports* from Mexico.

4. Damage from hub-and-spoke restrictions on Canadian imports from Mexico is likely to be more damaging to Canada's ability to compete in the future than at present.

Again, the story is similar. The amount of *present* Canadian imports from Mexico that would remain restricted in a hub-and-spoke but not in an FTA is relatively small ($1.6 billion in 1989, less auto pact imports that would be unrestricted in any case). But with the growth in Canadian income and demand for imports, along with an increasing Mexican supply capacity, a hub-and-spoke restriction of *future* Canadian imports could have a much more substantial effect in limiting the ability of Canadian firms to compete.

Thus the question posed in the first paragraph of this chapter can now be answered: The choice of trade regime *does* matter, but it is not so much because of how it affects present trade as how it affects potential future trade.

5. The last two hub-and-spoke problems for Canada apply equally to Mexico.

Because, in their two-way trade, Canada's exports are Mexico's imports and Canada's imports are Mexico's exports, hub-and-spoke restrictions on these two trade flows raise the same problems for Mexico.

While Canadian-Mexican two-way trade can be expected to grow more rapidly under an FTA than under a hub-and-spoke system, that trade should be kept in perspective. It is now, and is essentially certain to remain, far less significant than the huge bilateral trade flows between Canada and the United States and between Mexico and the United States. Nonetheless, Canada-Mexico trade is still important, not only because of its rapidly growing potential, but also because decisions taken on that trade today will set a pattern for extending free trade throughout the hemisphere.

6. Because their trade with the United States will continue to dominate their trade with each other, competition between Canada and Mexico will be concentrated less in the market of either than in the U.S. market.

Canadian opponents of free trade with Mexico argue that Canada should stay out of the Mexican free trade negotiations to avoid having to compete with Mexican goods in the Canadian market. But Canadians cannot avoid facing stronger competition from Mexican goods regardless of whether they participate in a trilateral agreement or allow Mexico and the United States to sign a bilateral. In either case, the competition from Mexico that Canada will have to face in the U.S. market will, as noted earlier, increase because the preference Canada acquired over Mexico in the U.S. market under the Canada-U.S. FTA will disappear.

A more important consideration for Canada is that it must *get into* the Mexican free trade negotiations in order to insure Canadian firms against damage to their ability to compete in the U.S. market. As the data in this chapter confirm, the U.S. market will be the most critical locale for Canadian and Mexican firms to compete.

Chapter Six

Where Should We Be Going?
The Interests of Canada, Mexico, and the United States

The theory of overlapping free trade areas (FTAs) — and, in particular, the comparison of a hub-and-spoke system with an FTA — developed in previous chapters could be applied to any of the world's hemispheres or, for that matter, to any group of countries. In this chapter, it is applied to the Western Hemisphere, drawing on the evidence on hemispheric trade set out in Chapter 5, and focusing on the interests of the three countries in North America that began negotiating a trilateral FTA in June 1991. In comparing this FTA with the hub-and-spoke system that would result from a bilateral between the United States and Mexico, the U.S. interest is the most difficult to clarify and is examined last.

It should be re-emphasized that all three countries have a common interest in an expanding FTA for all the reasons set out in Chapter 4. Compared with a hub-and-spoke, it would generate a larger potential increase in income and growth and it would avoid or minimize the abuses that would mark a hub-and-spoke regime, such as excess transport and administrative costs and rent-seeking waste — all of which would become even more costly in the almost certain event that the spoke bilaterals were inconsistent.

The Interests of Canada, the Existing Spoke

Canada, as the existing spoke, would prefer an FTA for two reasons set out in Chapter 3.

First, an FTA would give Canada better access to the Mexican market, by removing Mexican tariffs and by preventing discrimination there against Canadian exports. To illustrate how important access to the Mexican market may be, the number of telephone lines in Mexico is projected to double in the next five years. This is a new opportunity for Canadian producers of this equipment who for many years were unable to sell in Mexico. However, due to recent reforms, Canadian exporters, led by Northern Telecom with several cellular telephone equipment contracts, have increased their sales in Mexico from $5 million to $25 million in the first six months of 1990. And this is before the Mexican economy has seen any boost from free trade.

The second advantage for Canada of an FTA is that it would allow duty-free imports from Mexico that would benefit Canadian consumers and keep Canadian producers more competitive.

The Canadian Adjustment to Mexican Free Trade

While an FTA would benefit Canadian firms using inexpensive imports from Mexico, it would create a problem for Canadian firms competing with these imports. Would not one advantage for Canada of a hub-and-spoke system that leaves protection between Mexico and Canada intact be lower costs of adjusting to Mexican competition? The problem is that this is only a temporary advantage, since it would be blocking the trilateral free trade adjustment to an internationally more efficient allocation of resources, with the permanently higher productivity and income that this implies.

Moreover, much of the Canadian adjustment will be required whether or not there is Mexico-Canada free trade, since Canadian firms will have to adjust to the more competitive conditions in the U.S. market created by the Mexico-U.S. free trade that will be occurring in any case, and that will eliminate Canadian preference in the U.S. market over Mexico. It should be re-emphasized that it is in this U.S. market, rather than in the Canadian market, that Canadian firms will face the strongest competition from Mexico. In the U.S. market, Canadian exporters are competing with about $28 billion of annual Mexican exports. In the Canadian market, they are competing with only about $1.6 billion of Mexican exports. In short, opting for a hub-and-spoke by rejecting free trade with Mexico will not insulate Canada from the requirement to adjust to stiffer Mexican competition, since Canadian firms will still have to adjust to this in the U.S. market, where it matters most. And a hub-and-spoke system will make *that* adjustment more difficult because Canadian producers will be unable to acquire duty-free inputs from Mexico. Thus, it is not clear at all that adjustment would be less difficult for Canada under a hub-and-spoke system than under a trilateral FTA.

Although Mexican competition in Canada in an FTA will be relatively unimportant, it cannot be assumed away, especially because its absolute importance will surely increase over time. But it must be kept in perspective.

Moreover, when we examine one important dimension of that Mexican competition in Canada, automotive equipment, more than 90 percent of Canadian imports from Mexico already enters Canada duty free.[1] Although that figure, like any other on duty-free trade, may be biased upward, it is still very large and indicates that there may be little effect from tariff removal on the rest of this trade. In addition, much of the expansion of Mexican auto production may be in entry-level vehicles, and the big losers from this expansion may be the entry-level producers in Asia, rather than producers in Canada and the United States.[2]

To the degree that the impact of Mexican competition falls less on existing employment in Canada and more on the pattern of future employment, this competition will discourage future expansion of Canadian employment in low-productivity, low-wage jobs. It will therefore drive the Canadian employment structure upward into higher-productivity, higher-income activities in a relatively painless way, precisely because it is mostly an adjustment of future, rather than present, employment. This pressure on Canadian industry to move technologically upward while allowing Mexico to supply inexpensive products could be one of the major benefits of free trade with Mexico.

---

1 Some of these duty-free imports come into Canada under temporary duty-remission programs that will be expiring in 1995, but most come in under provisions of the Canada-U.S. auto pact.

2 This conclusion is supported by a recent study on the auto industry by Linda Hunter, James Markusen, and Tom Rutherford, "Trade Liberalization in a Multi-national-Dominated Industry: A Theoretical and Applied General Equilibrium Analysis," NBER Working Paper (Cambridge, Mass.: National Bureau of Economic Research, April 1991).

A Special Canadian Concern about a Hub-and-Spoke System

Canadians should consider the following disquieting possibility.[3] Suppose that a hub-and-spoke system is established by the signing of a Mexico-U.S. bilateral. There is no guarantee that such a system will continue to develop one country at a time. Instead, it may develop in blocs. To illustrate, suppose an FTA were to be created by a number of South American countries. (An example might be the free trade agreement that Argentina, Brazil, Paraguay, and Uruguay have recently signed and are scheduled to implement in 1995.) Suppose further that such an FTA were then to negotiate a spoke bilateral with the United States. With Canada then left as an outsider to the new large U.S.-South American spoke bilateral, all the hub-and-spoke problems described so far that Canada would face would apply in spades.[4] The discrimination and competitive problems Canada would face would be far worse than even those it would face in a hub-and-spoke system in which each of these same South American countries were an individual spoke.[5] Just preclud-

---

3 See Richard G. Lipsey, *Canada at the U.S.-Mexico Free Trade Dance: Wallflower or Partner?*, C.D. Howe Institute Commentary 20 (Toronto: C.D. Howe Institute, 1990), p. 12.

4 For example, Canadian exporters would not just face the discrimination described above in the Mexican market in competition with the United States; in addition, they would also face discrimination in each of the markets covered by the South American free trade agreement. Moreover, Canada would not just suffer in competition with the United States because that country could get inexpensive imports from Mexico; instead, Canada would suffer in competition with the United States and all the participating South American countries, because they would all be getting inexpensive imports (not available to Canada) from each other.

5 If the whole South American FTA were to be one spoke, Canadian exporters would be discriminated against in any South American market — say, Brazil — in competition not only with the United States, but with all other South American FTA members as well. On the other hand, if *each* of these South American countries were to be an individual spoke, then Canada would be discriminated against in, say, the Brazilian market only in competition with the United States.

It has been suggested that a group of South American countries should form an FTA before approaching the United States about free trade. As the argument above implies, that could raise serious problems if their new FTA were to become a spoke to the U.S hub. However, these problems would not arise if they were to seek inclusion in an expanding hemispheric free trade area.

ing this damaging possibility is arguably a sufficient reason for Canada to opt now for an expanding hemispheric FTA over a hub-and-spoke system.

To put this point in the simplest possible terms, if a country decides not to participate in an expanding FTA, there are an almost infinite number of damaging ways in which it can be "left out" as trade liberalization spreads through the hemisphere. This means that Canadians may have little choice. It does not matter whether they think participating in an expanding hemispheric FTA would benefit Canada or not. As long as the United States, Mexico, and possibly other countries are going ahead, it is worse for Canada to stay out than to participate. In this important economic respect, it is like the Uruguay Round. It did not matter whether Canadians liked it or not; it would have been worse to stay away.[6] Both cases have one thing in common: the high cost of being an outsider when trading partners are liberalizing their trade.

Another Advantage of an FTA for Canada: To Avoid the "Sideswipe" Problem

So far, in discussing Canada's interests, it has been assumed that any new spoke bilateral between the United States and, say, Mexico would be consistent with the existing Canada-U.S. bilateral. But suppose it is not. In that case, Canada would have an even stronger interest in a trilateral FTA, because it would thereby avoid being "sideswiped" by some special provisions in a Mexico-U.S. bilateral.

Such a sideswipe may be simple and obvious — for example, if Mexico negotiates a reduction in some U.S. nontariff barrier that provides it with better access to the U.S. market than Canada received in its FTA. In this case, Canada would be discriminated against in the U.S. market in competition with Mexico. In the Canada-U.S. negotiations, Canadian negotiators seemed to foresee

---

6 While most Canadian viewed the Uruguay Round as potentially beneficial, some undoubtedly did not. But there was no substantial objection raised to it, with one possible — perhaps partial — explanation being that those who did not like it viewed the alternative of staying away as worse.

this problem; they tried to ensure that Canada would automatically receive any benefits that the United States might extend to any other country. The United States, however, was not prepared to accept this constraint. Accordingly, this now becomes an important reason for Canada to trilateralize the negotiations with Mexico.

Alternatively, a sideswipe from a Mexico-U.S. bilateral could be far less simple and obvious, but just as damaging. An example could occur if, in the Mexican-U.S. negotiations, the Maquiladora issue is not appropriately dealt with. Under this program, Mexican exporting firms can acquire duty-free imports from any country. In a Mexico-U.S. free trade bilateral, Mexican firms would automatically acquire duty-free imports *from the United States*. In this limited sense, "all Mexico would become Maquila." However, the duty-free privilege of Maquiladora firms to import Japanese and other third-country imports for further processing and export to the United States would have to be ended, just as duty drawbacks were ended in the Canada-U.S. FTA. Otherwise, these Maquiladora producers would achieve a form of special preference in the U.S. market over U.S. producers — namely, the ability to purchase duty-free Japanese inputs for processing in goods sold in the United States. If this special privilege is not ended, it is easy to see how this negotiating failure could lead to a serious distortion of trade and investment in Mexico's favor, as production would be set up in Mexico to exploit this advantage. Moreover, Mexico would get this special advantage not only over U.S. producers, but also over Canadian exporters to the United States who would also be unable to acquire Japanese inputs duty free. In this case, Canada would be sideswiped not by any provision in the Mexico-U.S. bilateral, but instead by something far more difficult to discern: the *lack* of a provision necessary to amend the existing trade laws of Mexico.[7]

---

7 For further complications in any negotiation with Mexico and economic reasons why it would be in Canada's interest to participate — in addition to the importance of keeping the United States from developing a hub-and-spoke system — see Lipsey, *Canada at the U.S.-Mexico Free Trade Dance*; and Ronald J. Wonnacott, *Canada and the U.S.-Mexico Free Trade Negotiations*, C.D. Howe Institute Commentary 21 (Toronto: C.D. Howe Institute, 1990).

An Expanded FTA Would Provide
Better Trade and Political Balance

Canadian nationalists might prefer the addition of Mexico to an expanding free trade area — possibly with the potential later for addition of other Latin American countries — because it would provide some counterbalance to the weight and influence of the United States in the Canada-U.S. FTA. Indeed, free traders might join nationalists in preferring an expanding FTA not only because it would add such balance, but also because it would prevent the United States from acquiring an even more dominant economic role in the Americas than it will have, in any case, because of its economic size.

The increased dominance of the United States under a hub-and-spoke follows from the structure of the trading system itself — in particular, from the preferential economic advantage the United States would acquire. It should be emphasized that this increased U.S. dominance follows even if that country makes no attempt to exploit the special bargaining advantages it would acquire in a hub-and-spoke. But if it does choose to use those bargaining advantages, its dominance may be increased even further. Specifically, as the hub, the United States might be able to put a great deal of pressure on one spoke country at a time through threatened modification or reinterpretation of its bilateral agreement with that country. Thus, it might be able to increase its influence, both economically and politically, over the spoke countries.

This is, in essence, an extension of the problem noted in 1972 by then Canadian Minister of External Affairs Mitchell Sharp. Once a relatively small country has adjusted to a bilateral FTA with the United States by scaling up its industry to service the huge U.S. market, it becomes dependent on that market. It then has far more to lose than the United States from the termination of the FTA — or even from a less substantial shock to it.

Accordingly, mild U.S. threats about the possibility of termination or reinterpretation could put a great deal of pressure on Canadian business and the Canadian government. In short, the Sharp thesis is that explicit or implicit threats would give the United States a bargaining lever that would be very difficult for Canada to resist and might conceivably be exercised to influence its policy in quite unrelated noneconomic areas.

In Canada, the response to this has been: True, because of the FTA, a more open Canadian economy would be more vulnerable to U.S. trade action.[8] However, the FTA makes such U.S. action less likely, since it imposes greater constraints on the United States. Moreover, in the face of U.S. threats, Canada might draw on counter threats of its own. For example, it holds a substantial reserve of oil and other resources that will be in heavy future demand by U.S. industry. Termination of the FTA would end its conditional assurance of Canadian oil supplies to the U.S. market. In addition, the Canadian government, in its tax policies, exercises considerable control over U.S. investment in Canada. Thus, while the United States may hold Canadian markets hostage, Canada holds U.S. sunk capital. If the United States were to consider trade restraints, Canada could consider increasing its tax on foreign investment. Thus, the Canadian defense would be a credible threat of damage to U.S. interests. (No one would suggest that Canada — or, for that matter, the United States — would benefit from such an economic war, or even the threat of it. The point here is that Canada would have some defense.)

It is not clear that other spoke countries would have as effective a response to U.S. pressure — although the risk of political instability in those countries could be a strong deterrent to any U.S. threat of trade action. Accordingly, the U.S. bargaining position against these countries could become very strong. The fact that the United States would have a separate bilateral with each of its smaller partners might give them little chance, even in areas of common interest, to exercise collective pressure on, or resistance to, the United States. Certainly, they would have less opportunity than in an umbrella free trade agreement.

Thus, it is possible that, because of the bargaining power a hub-and-spoke system would give the United States, Latin Americans — in particular, Mexicans — might come to view that system as a means by which the United States might extend its hegemony over the hemisphere.

8 See Ronald J. Wonnacott, *Canada's Trade Options* (Ottawa: Economic Council of Canada, 1975), pp. 97–98.

The Interests of Mexico, the New Spoke

A concern that the United States would have a greater opportunity
to extend its economic and political hegemony over the hemisphere
is not the only objection to a hub-and-spoke that Mexico would have
in common with Canada.

Mexico's Long-Term Interests Are the Same as Canada's

Once Mexico, through a bilateral with the United States, becomes
a new spoke, *it would find itself in exactly the same situation as
Canada* when the United States considers further bilateral agreements with, say, Chile or Venezuela. In particular, it would face the
same problems cited above that Canada would now face if the United
States were to sign a bilateral with Mexico. These problems will not
be described again, but Mexicans should give them thoughtful
consideration.

It is very important for Mexicans to understand fully these
reasons for rejecting a hub-and-spoke system, since there are
several current pressures that may make a spoke bilateral seem
relatively attractive. One apparent short-run advantage is that a
bilateral may be a quicker way for Mexico to get a free trade
agreement with the United States. And time is now important — the
Mexican government wants to close an agreement well before its
next elections to be able to point to how the free trade agreement
may, by that time, have stimulated investment commitments by
foreigners and Mexicans repatriating capital.

While Mexico seems to have been originally motivated by the
desire to keep the negotiations quick and simple, it is not entirely
clear that a bilateral is a much better way of doing that than a
trilateral including Canada. True, the Canadian presence will tend
to make the negotiations more difficult and time consuming, simply
because another party is at the table. However, it may be easier to
negotiate by starting with the framework of the existing Canada-U.S.
FTA provisions, rather than starting from scratch to create a new
Mexico-U.S. agreement. Indeed, it can be argued in the European
Community (EC) case that, for new applicants, negotiating acces-

sion to the existing agreement has simplified and hastened, rather than delayed, their acquisition of free trade with the EC.

Another pressure on the Mexicans to choose the bilateral route has already been noted: it offers a greater opportunity to tailor U.S.-Mexico free trade to Mexico's special needs. One reason that Mexicans may view this as important is that Mexico may face substantial adjustment costs because it is a very small economy relative to the United States. In particular, its per capita income and productivity are relatively low. While this means that the free trade expectation is that Mexico will acquire large percentage gains in productivity and income — much larger than for Canada in its FTA with the United States — the other side of the coin is that this rapid economic change in Mexico may bring substantial costs of adjustment. This problem can, however, be dealt with in a trilateral agreement. Such an agreement can provide temporary relief, in particular by phasing in the reduction of Mexican trade barriers.

If, however, Mexico goes beyond seeking such special temporary adjustment provisions — and a limited class of other special provisions described in the next chapter that can also be accommodated in a trilateral agreement — to press for a bilateral U.S.-Mexico agreement permanently tailored to its special needs, it should understand how injurious such a precedent could be. If the United States continues to extend its free trade domain with a sequence of such bilaterals, rather than within the discipline and consistency imposed by the expansion of an FTA, what is to prevent it from offering some other Latin American countries better access to its market than Mexico may have been able to negotiate? As a hypothetical example, the United States might provide such better market access for, say, Chile, perhaps as an implicit form of assistance if a high oil price were to put Chile at a severe disadvantage *vis-à-vis* Mexico. However, were the price of oil to come down again, Mexico's advantage would disappear, and it would be left facing continued discrimination in the U.S. market in competition with Chile.

Concluding Remarks

Mexico, then, should welcome the Canadian presence in the trilateral negotiations. It should support Canada's role in setting a precedent for the role Mexico will be playing in future extensions of free trade throughout the Americas. In particular, Canada's participation in negotiating an expanded free trade area will set a precedent for similar Mexican participation in an expanding FTA later and ensure that the United States will not be expanding a hub-and-spoke system. Canada's protection of its interests to ensure that it is not sideswiped by new partner Mexico getting a better deal in the U.S. market will set a precedent for Mexico to protect itself from such a sideswipe in future negotiations with additional new partners. And just as Mexico provides some limited counterbalance for Canada in its FTA with the United States, Canada will provide a limited counterbalance for Mexico in its free trade with the United States.

The Interests of the U.S. Hub

The theory of preferential trading presented in Chapter 3 led to the conclusion that the hub would be the clearest beneficiary of a hub-and-spoke system because of the special preferential benefits it would acquire. However, in Chapter 4 it became evident that participant countries, including the hub, would face problems in a hub-and-spoke system that would not exist in an FTA — in particular, lost potential income due to a whole set of inefficiencies. Accordingly, at this point, it is no longer clear that even the U.S. hub would consider a hemispheric hub-and-spoke to be in its interests. This chapter now adds further grounds for U.S. skepticism in the form of special problems that the United States alone would face.

The Downside Cost to the United States of Its Special Benefits in a Hub-and-Spoke System

There is a cost to the United States from the special preference — that is, "export protection" — that its industry would acquire in spoke markets. Like protection in its domestic market, this protection of its exports may leave U.S. industry under less pressure to adjust to competition beyond the hemisphere, and thus less competitive in world markets. While it cannot be argued that this alone could justify a rejection of the preferential benefits of a hub-and-spoke, it is nonetheless a potential downside cost.[9]

Another downside cost is that the United States would be getting these preferential benefits only because each partner country (spoke) would be providing it with protection by discriminating against other partners. This is important not only from an economic but also from a political and foreign policy point of view.

Foreign Policy Complications in a Hub-and-Spoke System

With gains from an expanding FTA, and a dominant role in the Americas assured in any case by the size of its economy, it is not in the United States' foreign policy interest to be perceived as attempting to increase this dominance through a trading structure that would leave markets in the Americas carved up into a patchwork of what the United States would view as preferences, but that its partner countries would justifiably view as discrimination. The fact that under a hub-and-spoke (compared with an FTA) the United States would be benefiting at the expense of its partners in the Americas would give the charge of U.S. exploitation a credibility it does not otherwise deserve.

Moreover, there might well be unpredictable economic costs down the road if its partners, seeing the United States develop a special preferential position, were to seek to take some collective defensive action — perhaps even action that would be damaging. It is possible, for example, that by invoking a fair trade, level-playing-field defense, the U.S. partners might take some protectionist action that would damage both the United States and themselves. The problem is that the level-playing-field argument, so often abused in

---

9 There is another cost to the United States that alone would not justify rejecting a hub-and-spoke system but would nonetheless raise problems. Because the United States would be getting low-cost imports from spoke countries, it would have to face the temporary costs of adjusting to these inexpensive imports. (It would have to face this problem in an expanding FTA as well, but the burden would be less since it would be shared with its other FTA partners who would also be freely importing these low-cost goods.)

other contexts,[10] would have validity here as a criticism of the United States, since the *trading system itself* would, by inadvertence or design, have been structured to provide the United States with a special advantage over its partners.

A Hub-and-Spoke System and U.S. Protectionism

There are two important concerns about the possible growth of U.S. protectionism in a hub-and-spoke system.

Would a hub-and-spoke system damage the United States' incentive to pursue multilateral free trade?

Americans have always had an incentive for pursuing multilateral free trade (MFT) because, if it *could* be achieved, it would not only provide the highest real income for the world as a whole, but would also benefit the United States.[11] However, if a hub-and-spoke system were to be established, that second U.S. incentive to pursue MFT would be weakened, because under MFT the United States would have to give up the special preferential benefits it would get as the hub. Such a changing U.S. attitude could be damaging for the future of the world trading system, because the initiating and supporting role of the United States has been critical in the past pursuit of MFT.

---

10 Two examples of this abuse would be the arguments that (1) Mexico should continue to protect itself against the United States because higher U.S. productivity would mean that Mexico would not be competing on a level playing field; and (2) the United States should continue to protect itself against Mexico because low Mexican wages would mean that U.S. firms would not be competing on a level playing field.

11 This benefit to the United States holds under standard assumptions, including the assumption that the United States would not be damaged by an adverse change in its terms of trade, or at least the weaker assumption that any such damage would not be sufficient to offset U.S. benefits from MFT. This weaker assumption would be difficult to defend if the United States were the only country with terms-of-trade influence. But it is less difficult in a world in which both Europe and Japan have similar influence.

Would a hub-and-spoke system lead to a new, extended form of U.S. protectionism?

Even at present, it is difficult enough for the U.S. authorities to resist the pressure from strong lobbies seeking protection for U.S. firms in the domestic U.S. market. If some of the most substantial U.S. trading relationships were to be carved up into a hub-and-spoke regime, it might become even more difficult to resist a new, extended form of U.S. protectionism that would seek to protect U.S. firms against foreign competition, not just in the domestic market as always, but *also in the markets of spoke countries* where U.S. exporters would be protected by preferential treatment. This new form of protectionism by producers in the hub country might be called "domestic-export protectionism".

The problem with any such new U.S. protectionism is that it may be able to disguise itself as free trade easily and persuasively, precisely because it would be the defense of a policy (a U.S.-centered hub-and-spoke regime) that would include a substantial free trade element — namely, the removal of barriers to U.S. trade with spoke countries.[12] Thus, U.S. protectionists seeking to maintain the hub-and-spoke system would argue that they would not be defending protection at all, but just existing free trade agreements.

What would be wrong with this domestic-export protectionism? The answer is that, once a hub-and-spoke system is in place, U.S. business may want to defend it, even though for economic and foreign policy reasons the United States has an interest instead in the development of a hemispheric FTA and the continued support of multilateral free trade. The problem is that, on this issue, as on so many others in international trade, the interests of producers and the nation as a whole do not coincide. Business is unlikely to take into account the broad economic and foreign policy disadvan-

---

12 Both this problem and the preceding one of a reduced incentive for MFT also arise in an FTA, but to a less substantial degree, because the preferences created by an FTA are far less pervasive. For example, the problem of export protectionism arises in an FTA, and there have been examples of producers viewing the main point of an FTA as the protection they receive against third-country competition in partners' markets. But this problem would be even more serious in a hub-and-spoke system, because the U.S. hub would get much greater protection in partners' markets than it would in an FTA.

tages of a hub-and-spoke system. Instead, it would be likely to be concerned only with its existing domestic and export interests, and might therefore try to keep the hub-and-spoke system in place.

Would the U.S. government and its agencies be able to prevent the development of this new protectionism? It may depend on how far the hub-and-spoke process has gone. Before a hub-and-spoke system has been established, it may be relatively easy to get U.S. firms to support an FTA instead. Many will not recognize the difference in the two regimes, and those who do may favor an FTA because it provides a broader attack on trade barriers and therefore gives them greater freedom in internationalizing their operations. From the point of view of establishing efficient production in many countries, a U.S. multinational will prefer an FTA. There are already reports of this sort of support for an expanded FTA. Thus, *before* a hub-and-spoke regime has developed, U.S. firms may well judge an FTA to be superior.

It is *after* a hub-and-spoke system has become well established that their view may change. With their operations internationalized around this very special trading configuration, U.S. firms may become reluctant to give up the protection such a regime provides in export markets. Moreover, the larger the number of spokes that have been established, the more difficult it may be to get U.S. firms to give up this protection. Preventing the development of this new form of U.S. protectionism is another compelling reason for setting the right precedent now by negotiating a trilateral FTA with Mexico.

To sum up, even if there were only two spokes — Canada and Mexico — there are three reasons for pessimism about Washington's ability to contain this new protectionism:

- It is becoming increasingly difficult to resist even traditional U.S. protectionism.
- It is not clear that U.S. authorities will have sufficient will to resist a hub-and-spoke system, because, once established, this provides special benefits for U.S. business.
- Even those in the United States who, for broader reasons, view multilateral free trade and/or an expanding free trade area as more desirable may have difficulty in resisting the new U.S. protectionism because of its ability to masquerade as free trade.

The Problem of Choosing
the Next Bilateral Partner

A final U.S. concern should be what would happen if there were to be more applicants for a U.S. bilateral than U.S. negotiating resources could accommodate. The United States would then be forced to discriminate (saying yes to some countries, no to others) in offering a negotiation that would itself be discriminatory — an outcome that would be unsatisfactory from the point of view of both the United States and its potential partners.

Conclusion: Where Do We
Want to Go in the Hemisphere?

The answer to this question is that our objective should be to create a hemispheric FTA. The last four chapters lead to the conclusion that a hub-and-spoke development would be decidedly inferior for an existing spoke — in the present context, Canada — and for a new spoke — Mexico. Moreover, it is difficult to argue that it would provide net economic benefits even to the U.S. hub. True, it would provide the United States with special preferences. But these preferences would have two effects. First, they would increase the U.S. share of the North American income pie. Second, they would restrict the size of that pie. To put this last point more precisely, because these preferences would be based on trade distortions — that is, remaining trade barriers between spokes — the resulting inefficiency would make growth in the North American income pie smaller than it would be in an FTA. For the United States to choose a hub-and-spoke system that would restrict the size of the income pie while carving out a larger share for itself would be inappropriate for the nation that already has the highest income in the hemisphere. Moreover, the hub-and-spoke inefficiencies that would restrict the growth in the North American income pie would also limit U.S. income growth, leaving it far from clear that even the United States would, on balance, be left economically better off than under an FTA. This skeptical view of U.S. prospects draws further support from the broad noneconomic disadvantages of a hub-and-spoke system cited in this chapter.

I believe it was never the explicit intention of the United States to institute a hub-and-spoke system with these sorts of flaws. Nor, when it is fully understood, would the United States wish to have such a system develop.

Chapter Seven

How to Get There:
Selected Observations on the Negotiations

The appropriate objective identified in this study — a trilateral Canada-Mexico-U.S. agreement to establish an expanding free trade area (FTA) rather than a hub-and-spoke format — is also the objective set by the three countries for their negotiations that began in June 1991. In this chapter, no attempt will be made to set out a detailed negotiating strategy; instead, the focus will be on a few broad guidelines that follow once the FTA objective has been established.

Stick with the Trilateral FTA: Do Not Settle for a Mexico-U.S. Bilateral

It is often assumed that if there are difficulties in negotiating a trilateral, a bilateral Mexico-U.S. agreement can be negotiated, and that the hub-and-spoke system can be transformed later into a trilateral by the simple negotiation of a third (Canada-Mexico) bilateral. But it would not be that simple, because the United States would have to participate in some way in this second-stage negotiation.[1] Even then, arguably the best the three countries could do

---

1 To extend the illustration in Box 2 (on p. 34), suppose there is a Canada-Mexico-U.S. FTA with a 50 percent rule of origin. A good with 25 percent Mexican, 25 percent U.S., and zero Canadian content could enter the United States duty free from either Canada or Mexico. If there is a U.S.-centered hub-and-spoke system, it could not. For example, it could not come in duty free from Canada under the Canada-U.S. bilateral, since it would have only 25 percent Canadian content.

Could it come into the United States duty free if Canada and Mexico were to negotiate a bilateral? The answer is no, for precisely the same reason — it has only 25 percent Canadian content. Thus, the transformation of a U.S.- centered hub-and-spoke system into a trilateral FTA cannot be accomplished by Canada and Mexico alone by closing the system with their own bilateral. The United States must also be a party to an agreement by changing its rule of origin to a 50 percent Canadian, Mexican, or U.S. content.

would be to arrive at the trilateral FTA that they could have negotiated in the first place.

This process would involve two sets of both negotiating and adjustment costs — the first set required by the Mexico-U.S. bilateral and the second by the later trilateralization. The most serious potential problem, however, would be the risk that the second-stage trilateralization might not occur, perhaps because the participants might view this of second-order importance relative to other, more pressing issues. Given the pressure on hemispheric liberalization because of developments that are making other regions such as the European Community (EC) more competitive, there may not be time for two-stage solutions, no matter how straightforward or ingenious. If the second stage is not completed, then trade liberalization in North America would be cast in a hub-and-spoke configuration, with all the problems this would raise in any further extension of free trade throughout the hemisphere.

Bilateral Overtures by New Applicants

The second broad principle is that all members of the expanding FTA should reject any overtures for a bilateral agreement from any excluded country. Here, the United States holds the key, since it is the most likely member country to be approached. The appropriate role of the United States is to indicate to a new applicant that it will not entertain the idea of a bilateral; instead, the option for the prospective new member is to apply for entry into the expanding FTA.

This would prevent new candidate countries from developing the inflated expectation that they will be able to cut a deal with the United States tailored to their specific requirements — an expectation that could seriously complicate negotiations. Such U.S. action would also ensure the first-best FTA outcome, since the hub-and-spoke proposal that would, at most, be second-best need never come into play. This may be viewed as a special bonus in a world in which second-best solutions must often be chosen because first-best solutions are, for one reason or another, not feasible. Here, the first-best solution is not only feasible; it can essentially be ensured by the United States.[2]

The United States should follow this principle equally in dealing with a single applicant or a bloc of applying countries, such as a possible South American FTA.

The Existing FTA
Should Not Be Reopened

The third important guideline is that the provisions of the existing FTA should not be substantially renegotiated every time a new applicant nation is to be included. This goes to the heart of a Mexican-U.S. observation, sometimes expressed during early talks in 1990, that "we're willing to include Canada in these negotiations provided, of course, that Canada is prepared to make concessions" — the implication being that Canada should be willing to renegotiate some provisions of the Canada-U.S. FTA. Why should changes not be made, since the Canada-U.S. FTA is not perfect and can be improved? One problem is that, if the Canada-U.S. FTA is reopened, changes will not necessarily be to liberalize trade; they may be a protectionist move away from free trade.[3]

There are other problems in reopening the Canada-U.S. FTA now, or perhaps the Canada-Mexico-U.S. FTA later. The negotiating costs would be increased and, more importantly, the renegotiation of provisions would drag an FTA into the political arena of the existing FTA partners. To illustrate, the unavoidable political dis-

---

2 An expanding FTA is a "first-best" outcome only in the limited hemispheric-wide context of this study. In a worldwide context, it would not be, since, under standard assumptions, multilateral free trade would be first-best. Accordingly, it is worth restating an earlier conclusion. The first priority should be to pursue multilateral free trade under the General Agreement on Tariffs and Trade. It is only because complete success in this area cannot be realistically expected in the foreseeable future that hemispheric free trade has become an appropriate policy, with this monograph examining the best way of achieving that goal.

3 It is this risk of reopening the Canada-U.S. FTA that has led one of the Canadian negotiators of that agreement to oppose Canadian participation in the Mexican negotiations. See the comments by Gordon Ritchie in Roderick Hill and Ronald J. Wonnacott, eds., *Free Trade with Mexico: What Form Should It Take?*, C.D. Howe Institute Commentary 28 (Toronto: C.D. Howe Institute, 1991), pp. 19–20.

turbance that might occur in Canada from bringing Mexico into the existing Canada-U.S. FTA should not be aggravated by substantially changing the terms of that agreement. Thus, it is not in the U.S. and Canadian interest now, nor in the Canadian, U.S., and Mexican interest later, to have the terms of their existing FTA reopened if doing so would exacerbate these problems. (The exceptional conditions under which elements of the agreement could be reopened are discussed later in this chapter.)

Indeed, ensuring that the existing FTA is not substantially reopened when new partners are added may well be more important for Mexico than for Canada. A Mexican government seeking to lock in reforms that cannot be easily reversed by future governments should put heavy weight on this. Does it *really* want a reopening of the Canada-Mexico-U.S. FTA every time a new partner is included, with the risk that it could trigger a heated domestic debate in Mexico and perhaps an attempt by a more protectionist Mexican government to compromise the FTA, or perhaps even withdraw from it?

These last two broad principles — refusal by existing FTA members to (1) entertain new applications for bilaterals or (2) substantially change an existing FTA — seem to be leading to the conclusion that Mexico should be joining the Canada-U.S. FTA with no special bilateral provisions allowed.

Can Nothing Be Done to Address Mexico's Special Concerns?

It should be possible, within a broad framework of leaving the Canada-U.S. FTA substantially unchanged, to make some limited concessions to satisfy Mexico's special objectives.

> *Bilateral agreements are possible on issues that, by their very nature, are bilateral.*

Although it is essential to maintain the trilateral framework in the Mexican negotiations, certain specific bilateral accords can still be accommodated on issues that, by their very nature, are bilateral and must remain so, no matter how many countries might be included in the future. Examples might be Mexico-U.S. agreements on migration or low-wage transborder services.[4] Such agreements would not contaminate the trading system with hub-and-spoke discrimination, since they would have no discriminatory effect on existing partner Canada or on any future partner. It is only on potentially discriminatory issues such as tariff removal that the trilateral binding need apply.

Could Mexico decline to participate in some of the provisions of the Canada-U.S. agreement?

A Mexican decision not to participate in certain Canada-U.S. FTA provisions would not create the hub-and-spoke problem of Mexican discrimination against Canadian exports. But while it would not contaminate the trading system with discrimination, it would represent a lost opportunity for trade liberalization. There is an even stronger reason for resisting — though, in my view, not necessarily absolutely precluding — such a development: it would cause the other important hub-and-spoke problem of inconsistency among agreements, with the inefficiency this implies.

What if Americans and Mexicans want to liberalize trade further than the Canada-U.S. FTA?

While this is not possible in tariffs — since they are already zero in the Canada-U.S. FTA — it could be possible in nontariff provisions. For example, the United States and Mexico might consider a more open access to government procurement contracts than now exists in the Canada-U.S. FTA. This would generate hub-and-spoke contamination of the trading system, since existing partner Canada — and perhaps future partners in Central or South America — would be discriminated against in such contracts.

To prevent this, such an increased liberalization would have to be extended to Canada (and eventually to any other partner countries). But extending it now to Canada would mean reopening the Canada-U.S. FTA, which, it has already been argued, should not be an option. However, it may be reasonable to do this under two

---

4 This study neither recommends nor rejects such policies, since they would raise complex issues that would take us too far afield; these policies simply illustrate how some issues are purely bilateral.

conditions. First, any change should further liberalize trade rather than protect.[5] Indeed, press reports on the three countries' agreement to trilateralize the negotiations in early February 1991 suggested that this guideline may already have been put in place. Second, any change must be acceptable to all existing members — as, for example, both the United States and Canada have already judged acceptable a "reopening" of their FTA to liberalize it by two rounds of accelerated tariff reductions in 1990 and 1991. Such reopening, subject to these two important restrictions, would allow the existing Canada-U.S. FTA to be improved — an important objective in itself.

There is no question that the unanimity requirement would make revisions to the existing agreement more difficult as more and more members are included. Accordingly, if and when smaller countries — say, a group of Central American ones — were to be included in the expanding FTA, any change in the existing agreement might not necessarily require the approval of all individual partner countries, but instead only the approval of the United States, Canada, Mexico, and this Central American bloc, with this bloc exercising only one vote rather than several.

In an important sense, the sequencing of trade liberalization in the hemisphere has been very fortunate: U.S.-Canada first, with the most important agreement, since it covers by far the largest trading relationship; and Mexico, the next largest trading country in the hemisphere, included next. This has minimized the pressure at each stage to change the existing agreement. To see this from another point of view, suppose that the first hemispheric FTA had been an agreement negotiated by the United States with Brazil or Chile or even Mexico. Expanding this agreement to include Canada might well have required a more substantial set of changes to accommodate the requirements of Canada-U.S. trade, the largest trade flow in the world.

---

5 As an illustration of how protectionist changes should be resisted, it will be important for the Canada-U.S. dispute settlement mechanism not to be weakened. Establishing an effective procedure for settling disputes between the three countries without diluting the Canada-U.S. mechanism may become one of the most substantial challenges facing the negotiators.

Might temporary bilateral provisions be acceptable?

Yes, provided that, in a clearly specified timetable, they would be phased out or phased into conformity with the provisions of the existing FTA. Although this would temporarily create hub-and-spoke characteristics in the trading system, they would disappear.

Conclusion:
An Overview of a Trilateral Accord

The result of a tripartite negotiation would be a core of central provisions in the existing Canada-U.S. FTA on which the three countries would agree. This would represent a new Canada-Mexico-U.S. FTA. It would be overlaid by a minimum of bilateral provisions on which only two countries could agree, with most of these to be phased out, or phased into conformity with the Canada-U.S. FTA.[6] As this were to happen, the tripartite accord would increasingly have its core of desirable FTA provisions dominate its undesirable bilateral hub-and-spoke provisions, with these latter provisions eventually, in an ideal world, limited to issues that are inherently bilateral.

---

6 See Michael Hart, *A North American Free Trade Agreement: The Strategic Implications for Canada* (Ottawa: Center for Trade Policy and Law and Institute for Research on Public Policy, 1990), p. 99; and Richard G. Lipsey, *Canada at the U.S.-Mexico Free Trade Dance: Wallflower or Partner?*, C.D. Howe Institute Commentary 20 (Toronto: C.D. Howe Institute, 1990), pp. 9–10. Lipsey's suggestion is to phase essentially everything into the core, over whatever time period may be necessary, perhaps even 50 or 75 years for the more contentious provisions.

Chapter Eight

Future Trade in the Americas

The Mexican challenge illustrates the importance of having a long-term vision — conceived in very specific terms — of how the trading system should develop before taking any *ad hoc* initiatives, no matter how reasonable and beneficial these may seem on the face of it.

A Vision of Trade in the Hemisphere

In his "Enterprise for the Americas", U.S. President George Bush expressed his vision of free trade from the Beaufort Sea to Cape Horn. But because this vision was not specified more precisely, this initiative was left open to a possible interpretation — a series of U.S. bilateral trade agreements with each applicant country — that could lead the hemisphere not into a free trade agreement, but instead into a discriminatory hub-and-spoke system.

It is true that, with the United States, Mexico, and Canada now committed to achieving a trilateral free trade agreement, this is not the present negotiating intention. It is still essential, however, to understand the economics of the alternative hub-and-spoke system. Only then can the three countries fully understand the damage from failing to achieve a trilateral agreement, and appropriately resist defaulting to a Mexico-U.S. hub-and-spoke bilateral.

It will be more difficult for Americans than for others in the hemisphere to understand what is wrong with a hub-and-spoke system, since, from a U.S. vantage point, such a system would be free trade in all directions. However, from the vantage point of each U.S. partner, this system would be free trade as it looks toward the United States, but a byzantine maze of discriminatory trade barriers as it looks in any other direction toward its other hemispheric trading partners. This would not be an equal opportunity partnership. The United States would acquire the benefits of free trade with all countries in the Americas, but they would acquire the benefits of free trade only with the United States.

Where, in the long run, does the United States want its initiative to lead? To this sort of hub-and-spoke system, or to a hemisphere-wide free trade area (FTA) in which *all* countries are trading freely in the hemisphere as they look out in *any* direction; in which all countries face the same trading rules, with none getting preferential treatment and none facing discrimination?

Given the wealth and size of the United States, there is no way that any trading system can make the countries in the Americas equal. But an FTA, unlike a hub-and-spoke, would provide them all, to the greatest degree possible, with *equal opportunity*. That is the very least that should now be offered to the less wealthy countries in the hemisphere. That is the best way to alleviate poverty in Latin America, and with it the problem of debt — and those objectives are not only in the interests of the Latin American countries, but of the United States as well.

In offering such an equal opportunity partnership, U.S. leadership will be welcomed. It will not be if, alternatively, the United States offers only spoke bilaterals. No matter how much bilaterals may initially be appreciated, that will fade as trading partners come to recognize the way in which, compared with an FTA, the resulting discriminatory system confers special benefits on the United States at their expense.

Thus, the U.S. vision of an FTA for the Americas is critical. It has been that sort of vision of a freely trading world that has led the United States to promote and support multilateral free trade. That is the way the world should trade; it is in the collective interest of all countries. Accordingly, the United States has not reduced its decision to support multilateral free trade to a calculation of whether — as a result of terms-of-trade effects or whatever — this sort of a world is actually in its own economic interest. As it looks out over the hemisphere, that is the sort of vision that the United States should continue to hold. An FTA is the way the hemisphere should trade. Thus, the United States should not reduce its decision to support an FTA to a calculation of whether — as a result of differences in preferences or whatever — such a system would actually be in its own economic interest.

Nonetheless, even if the United States *were* to reduce the decision to a narrow calculation of its own interest, this study concludes that it would still judge an expanding FTA to be, on balance, superior. It is very difficult to argue that the preferential advantages of a hub-and-spoke system would offset the costs, both direct and indirect, from its trade-distorting inefficiencies and its offensive noneconomic characteristics. This FTA vision is important for the United States because that country, more than any other, holds the negotiating key. As the recipient of applications by new countries for bilaterals, it is in a position to refuse, leaving them with the option of joining the existing FTA instead.

More Complex Hub-and-Spoke Possibilities?

The basic theory of overlapping bilaterals presented in Chapters 3 and 4 provides the key to analyzing more complicated hub-and-spoke systems that may be proposed in the future. For example, what would happen if the U.S. hub were to sign a bilateral with Japan? Those who are tempted to say it could never happen should remember that "never" used to be defined as "not within 50 years" — now it is six months. The deputy chief secretary of the Japanese Cabinet has warned that, without a free trade pact with the United States, Japan faces the danger of being excluded from regional blocs in Europe and North America.

If, through a Japan-U.S. bilateral, the United States were to extend its hub-and-spoke network across the Pacific, it would no longer be just carved-up trade in the Americas, with its important cumulative effect. With a Japanese bilateral, the United States would create a hub-and-spoke system right at the heart of world trade. The addition of this single Japanese spoke would have immediate, profound effects on Canada and any other existing U.S. partners.

The same is true of a U.S. bilateral with the European Community (EC), conceivably in manufactured goods. Even though this seems even less likely than a U.S. bilateral with Japan, it is a particularly interesting case on which to speculate, not just because of the size of the EC, but also because the EC is itself a hub in a very special hub-and-spoke regime. Thus, an EC-U.S. bilateral would make the United States a spoke in the EC wheel *and* the EC a spoke in the U.S. wheel.

Finally, consider the sort of trade relations that countries in Eastern Europe may seek. Might the EC make spoke agreements with several of these? Might Eastern European countries have hub-and-spoke agreements among themselves? The complexity of possible arrangements in this region would be greatly increased if the Soviet Union were to split up politically, with the resulting parts then seeking some form of trade arrangement with each other, with countries in Eastern Europe, and/or with the EC. Greater changes than this have occurred in this region in the past few years. It is possible that the trade map in this region could be completely redrawn by those who do not understand how markets work, let alone the subtleties of overlapping free trade areas.

Revising Traditional Beliefs about Free Trade Areas

This study has shown that the traditional economics of free trade areas applies so long as these areas do not overlap. If they do, however, a different economic analysis is required, and it is no surprise that some of the traditional principles of a free trade area no longer hold.

First, it has traditionally been believed that an FTA is preferable to a customs union because it allows each partner freedom to liberalize its trade with the rest of the world. While this remains true so long as each partner is liberalizing its trade unilaterally, problems arise if it is liberalizing its trade with third countries bilaterally or in any other reciprocal way. Then, the hub-and-spoke problems of overlapping free trade areas arise. To avoid these, there may be an advantage to having a "customs union discipline" whereby any new member is required to conform to the provisions of the existing members. Another advantage of a customs union is that it does not require rules of origin, which are becoming increasingly difficult to enforce.

Another commonly held belief — often cited in the Canada-U.S. case — is that an FTA has an advantage over multilateral trade liberalization because countries participating in an FTA can tailor the agreement to meet their own special needs. While such tailoring is an advantage so long as there is only one FTA, it has been shown that two problems arise if FTAs overlap. First, tailoring would create inconsistencies among FTAs that would exacerbate the inefficiencies that would arise even in a perfectly consistent set of agreements. Second, without adequate foresight, a potential new partner country might fall into a "tailoring trap" by failing to recognize that any advantage it may acquire from its own specially tailored agreement may be more than offset later by new partners being consequently able to tailor their agreements, and doing so at that country's expense.

Finally, it was traditionally believed that it was simple to add new partners to an FTA. This study has shown that it may not be simple at all.

Selected References

Bilateral Commission on the Future of United States-Mexican Relations. *The Challenge of Interdependence: Mexico and the United States.* Lanham, Maryland: University Press of America, 1988.

Camps, Miriam, and William Diebold, Jr. *The New Multilateralism.* New York: Council on Foreign Relations, 1986.

Cox, David, and Richard G. Harris. "A Quantitative Assessment of the Economic Impact on Canada of Sectoral Free Trade with the United States," *Canadian Journal of Economics* 19 (August 1986).

Diebold, William, Jr., ed. *Bilateralism, Multilateralism, and Canada in U.S. Trade Policy.* Cambridge, Mass.: Ballinger, 1988.

Hart, Michael. *A North American Free Trade Agreement: The Strategic Implications for Canada.* Ottawa: Center for Trade Policy and Law and Institute for Research on Public Policy, 1990.

Hill, Roderick, and Ronald J. Wonnacott, eds. *Free Trade with Mexico: What Form Should It Take?*, C.D. Howe Institute Commentary 28. Toronto: C.D. Howe Institute, 1991.

Hunter, Linda, James Markusen, and Tom Rutherford. "Trade Liberalization in a Multinational-Dominated Industry: A Theoretical and Applied General Equilibrium Analysis," NBER Working Paper. Cambridge, Mass.: National Bureau of Economic Research, April 1991.

Lipsey, Richard G. *Canada at the U.S.-Mexico Free Trade Dance: Wallflower or Partner?*, C.D. Howe Institute Commentary 20. Toronto: C.D. Howe Institute, 1990.

Morici, Peter. "The Implications for the Future of U.S. Trade Policy." In Peter Morici, ed. *Making Free Trade Work: The Canada-U.S. Agreement.* New York: Council on Foreign Relations, 1990.

Richardson, Martin. "Trade Diversion and Endogenous Tariff Formation." Washington, D.C., Georgetown University, Department of Economics, 1990, unpublished manuscript.

Schott, Jeffrey, ed. *Free Trade Areas and U.S. Trade Policy.* Washington, D.C.: Institute for International Economics, 1989.

Smith, Murray G. "The Mexico, United States and Canada Trade Talks: Getting Off on the Right Foot," Council on Foreign Relations Discussion Paper. New York: Council on Foreign Relations, 1990.

Vega Cánovas, Gustavo. "Las relaciones comerciales entre México y Estados Unidos." In Gustavo Vega Cánovas, coordinator. *México ante el libre comercio con America del Norte.* Mexico City: El Colegio de México and Universidad Tecnológica de México, 1991.

Viner, Jacob. *The Customs Union Issue.* New York: Carnegie Endowment for International Peace, 1950.

Weintraub, Sidney. *A Marriage of Convenience: Relations between Mexico and the United States.* New York: Oxford University Press, 1990.

Wonnacott, Ronald J. *Canada and the U.S.-Mexico Free Trade Negotiations,* C.D. Howe Institute Commentary 21. Toronto: C.D. Howe Institute, 1990.

———. "Canada's Future in a World of Trade Blocs: A Proposal," *Canadian Public Policy* 1 (Winter 1975): 118–130.

———. *Canada's Trade Options.* Ottawa: Economic Council of Canada, 1975.

Members of the
Canadian-American Committee

Co-chairmen

JOHN P. FISHER
President and Chief Executive Officer,
Southam, Inc., Toronto, Ontario

ROBERT G. NICHOLS
Partner, Price Waterhouse,
New York, N.Y.

Members

PETER A. ALLEN
Chairman, President and Chief
Executive Officer, LAC Minerals
Limited, Toronto, Ontario

JOHN R. ALTENAU
Vice-President, Manufacturers
Hanover Trust Co., New York, N.Y.

JACQUES BOUGIE
President and Chief Operating
Officer, Alcan Aluminium Limited,
Montreal, Quebec

DAVID I.W. BRAIDE
Chairman, Canadian Institute on
International Peace and Security,
Toronto, Ontario

PHILIP BRIGGS
Vice-Chairman, Metropolitan Life
Insurance Company, New York, N.Y.

RONALD F. BUDZIK
Vice-President, International and
Government Affairs, Mead
Corporation, Dayton, Ohio

BILL CASSTEVENS
Secretary-Treasurer, United Auto
Workers, Detroit, Michigan

PETER A. CHERNIAVSKY
Chairman, BC Sugar, Vancouver, B.C.

JOHN E. CLEGHORN
President and Chief Operating
Officer, The Royal Bank of Canada,
Montreal, Quebec

MARSHALL A. COHEN
President and Chief Executive Officer,
The Molson Companies Limited,
Toronto, Ontario

FREDERICK A. COPELAND
President, Citibank Canada,
Toronto, Ontario

EDWARD H. CRAWFORD
Chairman, Canada Life Assurance
Company, Toronto, Ontario

JAMES A. CURTIS
Chairman and Chief Executive
Officer, Milliman and Robertson Inc.,
Seattle, Washington

CHARLES DALE
President, The Newspaper Guild
(AFL-CIO, CLC), Silver Spring,
Maryland

WILLIAM DIEBOLD
Upper Nyack, N.Y.

CHARLES F. DORAN
Professor and Director, Center for
Canadian Studies, Johns Hopkins
University, School of Advanced
International Studies,
Washington, D.C.

The Hon. THOMAS ENDERS
Managing Director, Salomon Brothers
Inc., New York, N.Y.

HOWARD ENGLE
Partner, Arthur Andersen &
Company, Chicago, Illinois

STEPHEN C. EYRE
Executive Director, The John
Hartford Foundation, Inc.,
New York, N.Y.

KENT B. FOSTER
President, GTE Telephone
Operations, Irving, Texas

ROBERT FRANKLIN
President and Chief Executive Officer,
Ontario Hydro, Toronto, Ontario

WILLIAM C. GARRIOCK
President and Chief Executive Officer,
Miles Canada Inc., Etobicoke, Ontario

LEO GERARD
Director, District #6,
United Steelworkers of America,
Toronto, Ontario

HAYWARD R. GIPSON
Vice-President and General Manager,
Consumer International, Corning
Incorporated, Corning, N.Y.

PATRICK M. HALL
Vice-President, Rockwell
International, Arlington, Virginia

JAMES F. HANKINSON
President and Chief Operating
Officer, Canadian Pacific Limited,
Toronto, Ontario

JAMES M. HAY
Vice-Chairman, Dow Chemical
Canada Inc., Sarnia, Ontario

ARDEN R. HAYNES
Chairman and Chief Executive
Officer, Imperial Oil Limited,
Toronto, Ontario

LUTHER S. HELMS
Chairman and Chief Executive
Officer, Seattle First National Bank,
Seattle, Washington

FREDERICK E. HENNIG
President and Chief Operating
Officer, Woolworth Corporation,
New York, N.Y.

LEON HESS
Chairman and Chief Executive
Officer, Amerada Hess Corporation,
New York, N.Y.

EDGAR HOTARD
President, Union Carbide Industrial
Gases, Danbury, Connecticut

DAVID E. JACKSON
Executive Vice-President,
NALCO Chemical Company,
Naperville, Illinois

E. SYDNEY JACKSON
Vice-Chairman, The Manufacturers
Life Insurance Company, Toronto,
Ontario

JACK J. JACKSON
Vice-President, U.S. Pharmaceutical
Sales, The Upjohn Company,
Kalamazoo, Michigan

ERLAND KAILBOURNE
Chairman and Chief Executive
Officer, Norstar Bank, Buffalo, N.Y.

ROBERT KAVNER
Group Executive, Data Systems,
Federal Systems, AT&T,
Basking Ridge, N.Y.

OWEN J. NEWLIN
Senior Vice-President, Pioneer
Hi-Bred International Inc.,
Des Moines, Iowa

ANTHONY H. NEWTON
Vice-President, Commodities, Nabisco
Brands Inc., East Hanover, N.J.

JAMES R. NININGER
President and Chief Executive Officer,
The Conference Board of Canada,
Ottawa, Ontario

GORDON F. OSBALDESTON
Senior Fellow, School of Business
Administration, University of Western
Ontario, London, Ontario

JOHN PEPPER
President, The Proctor & Gamble
Company, Cincinatti, Ohio

JAMES E. PERRELLA
Executive Vice-President, Ingersoll
Rand Company, Woodcliffe Lake, N.J.

ROBERT L. PIERCE
Chairman and Chief Executive
Officer, Foothills Pipe Lines Ltd.,
Calgary, Alberta

JOHN W. PITTS
President and Chief Executive Officer,
MacDonald, Dettwiler & Associates
Ltd., Richmond, B.C.

GEORGE J. POULIN
General Vice-President, International
Association of Machinists and
Aerospace Workers, Northeast
Territory, Stamford, Connecticut

WILLIAM S. RANDALL
President and Chief Executive Officer,
First Interstate Bank of Arizona,
Phoenix, Arizona

SHELDON M. RANKIN
President, Marsh & McLennan
Limited, Toronto, Ontario

GORDON R. RITCHIE
Chief Executive Officer, Strategico
Inc., Ottawa, Ontario

DAVIS R. ROBINSON
LeBoeuf, Lamb, Leiby & MacRae,
Washington, D.C.

A.E. SAFARIAN
Centre for International Studies,
University of Toronto,
Toronto, Ontario

ANDRÉ SAUMIER
Chairman, Saumier Frères, Conseil,
Montreal, Quebec

JAMES R. SCHLESINGER
Senior Advisor, Lehman Brothers,
Washington, D.C.

GERALD SHEFF
Gluskin Sheff + Associates,
Toronto, Ontario

JACK SHEINKMAN
President, Amalgamated Clothing and
Textile Workers' Union, New York, N.Y.

CHARLES E. SHULTZ
President and Chief Executive Officer,
Gulf Canada Resources Limited,
Calgary, Alberta

JOHN C. SIENKIEWICZ
Senior Vice-President and Director,
Client Services, Alexander &
Alexander Inc., New York, N.Y.

HELEN SINCLAIR
President, The Canadian Bankers'
Association, Toronto, Ontario

RICHARD SONSTELIE
President Puget Sound Power and
Light, Bellevue, Washington

JOHN SWEENEY
President, Service Employees
International Union (AFL-CIO),
Washington, D.C.

W. PIKE TALBERT
Principal, Morgan Stanley Company
Inc., New York, N.Y.

MICHAEL THIENEMAN
President and Chief Executive Officer,
Inglis Limited, Mississauga, Ontario

R.J. (ROLY) THOMPSON
President, GSW Inc., Fergus, Ontario

JOHN TORY
Deputy Chairman, Thomson
Newspapers Corporation,
Toronto, Ontario

PETER M. TOWE
Chairman and Chief Executive
Officer, Petro-Canada International
Assistance Corporation,
Ottawa, Ontario

ROBERT vom EIGEN
Partner, Hopkins and Sutter,
Washington, D.C.

SIDNEY WEINTRAUB
Dean Rusk Professor, LBJ School of
Public Affairs, University of Texas at
Austin

GEORGE WEYERHAEUSER
Chairman, Weyerhaeuser Company,
Tacoma, Washington

DENNIS K. WILLIAMS
Chairman and Chief Executive
Officer, General Electric Canada Inc.,
Mississauga, Ontario

LYNN R. WILLIAMS
International President, United
Steelworkers of America (AFL-CIO,
CLC), Pittsburgh, Pennsylvania

BARRY WILSON
President, Intercontinental Division,
Bristol-Myers Squibb Co.,
Princeton, N.J.

LYNTON R. WILSON
President and Chief Operatinf Officer,
BCE Inc., Montreal, Quebec

CHARLES G. WOOTTON
Coordinator, International Public
Affairs, Chevron Corporation,
San Francisco, California

ADAM H. ZIMMERMAN
Chairman, Noranda Forest Inc.,
Toronto, Ontario

Honorary Member

M.W. MacKENZIE
Peterborough, Ontario

Sponsoring Organizations

The C.D. Howe Institute is an independent, nonprofit, research and educational institution. Its goals are to identify current and emerging economic and social policy issues facing Canadians; to analyze options for public- and private-sector responses; to recommend, where appropriate, particular policy options that, in the Institute's view, best serve the national interest; and to communicate the conclusions of its research to a domestic and international audience in a clear, nonpartisan way. While its focus is national and international, the Institute recognizes that each of Canada's regions may have a particular perspective on policy issues and different concepts of what should be national priorities.

The Institute was created in 1973 by a merger of the Private Planning Association of Canada (PPAC) and the C.D. Howe Memorial Foundation. The PPAC, formed in 1958 by business and labor leaders, undertook research and educational activities on economic policy issues. The Foundation was created in 1961 to memorialize the late Rt. Hon. Clarence Decatur Howe, who served Canada as Minister of Trade and Commerce, among other elected capacities, between 1935 and 1957. The Foundation became a separate entity in 1981.

The Institute encourages participation in and support of its activities from business, organized labor, associations, the professions, and interested individuals. For further information, please contact the Institute's Membership Coordinator.

Adam H. Zimmerman is Chairman, and Thomas E. Kierans is President and Chief Executive Officer. The Institute's offices are located at: 125 Adelaide Street East, Toronto, Ontario M5C 1L7 (tel. 416-865-1904; fax 416-865-1866); and P.O. Box 1621, Station "M", Calgary, Alberta T2P 2L7 (tel. 403-233-8044).

The National Planning Association (NPA) is an independent, private, nonprofit, nonpolitical organization that carries on research and policy formulation in the public interest. NPA was founded during the Great Depression of the 1930s when conflicts among the

major economic groups — business, labor, agriculture — threatened
to paralyze national decisionmaking on the critical issues confronting American society. It was dedicated to the task of getting these
diverse groups to work together to narrow areas of controversy and
broaden areas of agreement and to provide on specific problems
concrete programs for action planned in the best traditions of a
functioning democracy. Such democratic planning, NPA believes,
involves the development of effective governmental and private
policies and programs not only by official agencies but also through
the independent initiative and cooperation of the main private-sector groups concerned. And to preserve and strengthen American
political and economic democracy, the necessary government ac-
tions have to be consistent with, and stimulate the support of, a
dynamic private sector.

NPA brings together influential and knowledgeable leaders
from business, labor, agriculture, and the applied and academic
professions to serve on policy committees. These committees identify emerging problems confronting the nation at home and abroad
and seek to develop and agree upon policies and programs for coping
with them. The research and writing for these committees are
provided by NPA's professional staff and, as required, by outside
experts.

In addition, NPA's professional staff undertakes research designed to provide data and ideas for policymakers and planners in
government and the private sector. These activities include research
on national goals and priorities, productivity and economic growth,
welfare and dependency problems, employment and manpower
needs, and technological change; analyses and forecasts of changing international realities and their implications for U.S. policies;
and analyses of important new economic, social and political realities confronting American society. In developing its staff capabilities,
NPA has increasingly emphasized two related qualifications. First is
the development of the interdisciplinary knowledge required to
understand the complex nature of many real-life problems. Second
is the ability to bridge the gap between theoretical or highly technical
research and the practical needs of policymakers and planners in
government and the private sector.

All NPA reports are authorized for publication in accordance
with procedures laid down by the Board of Trustees. Such action

does not imply agreement by NPA board or committee members with all that is contained therein unless such endorsement is specifically stated.

NPA publications, including those of the Canadian-American Committee, can be obtained from the Association's offices, 1424-16th Street, N.W., Suite 700, Washington, D.C. 20036 (tel. 202-265-7685).